W9-AEK-920

CHARACTER BUILDERS
Responsibility and Trustworthiness

A K-6 CHARACTER EDUCATION PROGRAM

- Ready-to-Implement Character Building Activities
- Literature and Vocabulary Selections
- School or Classroom Character Theme Posters
- Puppets, Activities, and Stories Adapted for Younger Children with "Able," the Shooting Star
- A Character Thought for Each Day

Dr. Michele Borba

Jalmar Press

Character Builders: Responsibility and Trustworthiness

Jalmar Press
Permission's Department
P. O. Box 1185
Torrance, CA 90505
(310) 816-3085 Fax: (310) 816-3092 e-mail: blwjalmar@worldnet.att.net
Website: www.jalmarpress.com

Published by Jalmar Press

Character Builders: Responsibility and Trustworthiness
A K-6 Character Education Program

Author: Dr. Michele Borba
Editor and story writer: Marie Conte
Project Director: Jeanne Iler
Cover Design: Electronic Publishing Services, Inc., TN
Interior Design and Composition: Electronic Publishing Services, Inc., TN
Interior Illustrations: Bob Burchett

Manufactured in the United States of America

10 9 8 7 6 5 4 3 2 1
ISBN: 1-880396-54-8

Contents

Contents

5   Becoming a Responsible Learner   89

Introduction

Building Character in Students

It's great to be great, but it's greater to be human.
—Lucy M. Montgomery

In my consulting tours of school sites one experience became all too common. I'd walk into a classroom and notice a rule chart clearly posted with pre-established student expectations. Then I'd quietly walk up to a student, and choose one of the rules to quiz him on the meaning. The conversation generally went like this: "One of the rules on the chart says you are to act responsibly at this school. What does responsibility mean?" All too frequently the student's response would be a "shrug of the shoulders" or a simple "I don't know." I'd prod the student a bit further: "But it says you're supposed to act responsibly. Can you tell me what that looks like and sounds like?" "I don't know," the student would say.

What I just described is an all too common trend. Far too many of today's students do not know the meaning, behavior, and value of some of the most critical traits of solid character. And, there's a significant reason why: character traits, like skills, are learned. One of the primary ways students acquire these traits is by watching others do them right. Reflect on that statement a minute and ask yourself: "Who are my students watching to learn these traits?" Over the past few years we've witnessed a breakdown of appropriate role models for today's youth. Some of the primary sources that used to nurture the self-esteem of our students have broken down: the home, the neighborhood block, community support agencies, even the schools have become larger and less personalized. Role models for today's students are frankly atrocious. I watch in horror as a professional baseball player on national television is allowed to spit in an umpire's face and not be held accountable. I'm astounded when rock stars and authors of some of the most hateful lyrics I've ever heard receive standing ovations. I'm amazed that so many actors (some without even a high school diploma) are given contracts that quadruple the salary of the President of the United States. The breakdown of appropriate role models for our youth is clearly an enormous educational handicap.

The breakdown of appropriate role models is certainly not the only reason for the decline in solid character development of our youth. Dr. Thomas Lickona cites ten troubling trends among youth in our society that point to an overall moral decline. Over the past decades these ten indicators, which have been increasing significantly, show a failure of our students in the acquisition and development of character:

Youth Trends and Moral Decline

1. Violence and vandalism.

2. Stealing.

3. Cheating.

4. Disrespect for authority.

5. Peer cruelty.

6. Bigotry.

7. Bad language.

8. Sexual precocity and abuse.

9. Increasing self-centeredness and declining civic responsibility.

10. Self-destructiveness.

Dr. Thomas Lickona: Educating for Character. Bantam: 1991. p. 16-18.

> "Sow an act, and you reap a habit. Sow a habit, and you reap a character. Sow a character, and you reap a destiny."
>
> —Charles Reade

What can help turn these trends around? A recent poll revealed that 86% of adults surveyed believed that the number one purpose of public schools, apart from providing a basic education, is "to prepare students to be responsible citizens." (*Learning,* March/April 1997, page 3)

The truth is that school may well be the last beacon of hope for many of our students. How else will they have a chance to understand the value of traits called "responsibility" or "caring" or "respect" or "peacemaking" or "cooperation?" How else will these youths have the opportunity to watch someone model the trait appropriately? How else but at school will many of our students be able to learn these core skills of success, not only for school but in their life! Your power in your role of "educator" is extraordinary. The simple but profound truth is, How else but from a caring, committed teacher will many of today's students have a chance to expand their personal, social, and academic potential? This series, called *Character Builders,* will show you how.

Character Builders is purposely designed to be used in many ways. Each Character Builder can be infused into almost any subject. The themes have been carefully chosen based not only on research in character development but also in self-esteem theory. Each Character

Builder teaches students not only the trait but also a few core skills that will optimize their chances of success not only in school but also in life. The dream of educators is to have students who are more responsible, respectful, cooperative, peaceable and caring. Where do you begin? The key to enhancing student character development I believe is found in three critical premises. Above all else, keep these three premises in mind:

Premises of Character Development

- Character traits are learned.

- Character traits are changeable.

- Educators are able to create the conditions that enhance such change because they can control the learning environment and their attitude.

Let's analyze each one of these premises. Each one is important to understand if we want to enhance the character development of our students:

Character traits are learned. To the best of my scientific knowledge there are no genes for character development and self-esteem; none of our students are born with strong character. Instead, our children have acquired their character and self-esteem through repeated experiences in their pasts. Too often, the critical skills that enhance the core Character Builders have not been modeled or emphasized for students. You can make a difference for your students by deliberately modeling the traits and by providing them with opportunities to learn these skills.

"Show me the man you honor, and I will know what kind of man you are."

—Thomas Carlyle

Character traits are changeable. From the premise that character development is learned, a second principle arises naturally and unavoidably: If character traits are learned, therefore we can teach them and change them. It is essential to keep this concept in mind because it means that educators and parents do have tremendous power to teach critical skills and traits that optimize students' chances of success not only now but for the rest of their lives.

Educators are able to create the conditions that enhance such change because they can control the environment and their attitude. If character traits and skills are learned and changeable, then educators have the ability to create those changes by means of their attitudes, their curriculum content and the atmosphere they create. What is needed is the knowledge of what skills are most important to enhance each trait and which traits we should deliberately accentuate and model to help students "catch" the attitudes. That's what *Character Builders* is all about . . . and we haven't a moment to lose!

Character Builders is based on the same premises as *Esteem Builders: A K-8 Curriculum for Improving Student Achievement, Behavior and School Climate* that I published in 1989. The esteem-building series includes manuals for school, home, staff and workshop training, all designed to provide a comprehensive approach to developing high self-esteem in students. *Character Builders* is the next step in teaching students the skills that will help them succeed. The five core Character Builders complement the Esteem Builders for high self-esteem, namely: Security, Selfhood, Affiliation, Mission, and Competence. These five components serve as the foundation for enhancing students' positive self-perceptions, thereby encouraging the development of their potential and confidence in learning. The esteem building blocks have been sequenced within each character building theme to ensure that students will acquire these skills as well. It is strongly recommended that the themes within this manual be presented in the order in which they were written. This is the best way to ensure students' acquisition of the skills and character building traits. The five core Character Builders in this series are listed below along with their corresponding Esteem Builders.

Five Core Esteem and Character Builders

Esteem Builder Trait

Character Builder Trait

Security
A feeling of comfort and safety; being able to trust others.

Responsibility and Trustworthiness
Doing what is right; being answerable and accountable to yourself and others.

Selfhood
A feeling of individuality; acquiring an accurate and realistic self-description

Respect
Treating yourself and others in a courteous and considerate manner.

Affiliation
A feeling of belonging, acceptance or relatedness.

Cooperation
Respectfully working with others in a fair and equitable manner to accomplish mutual goals.

Mission
A feeling of purpose and motivation in life; setting achievable goals.

Peaceability
Solving conflicts in a peaceful and responsible manner; building solid citizenship skills.

Social Competence
A feeling of success when relationships are handled respectfully and responsibly.

Caring
Showing concern and sensitivity for the needs and feelings of others; being compassionate and empathetic.

The activities in this book have been organized around six core universal moral values outlined by a group of twenty-nine youth leaders and educators at what has come to be known as the "Aspen Conference." The six core values are:

"We don't know who we are until we see what we can do."

—Martha Grimes

- Trustworthiness

- Respect

- Responsibility

- Justice and Fairness

- Caring

- Civic Virtue and Citizenship

IMPLEMENTING THE PROGRAM

Character Builders is designed to be used in many ways, including:

- on a daily or month-by-month or bi-monthly basis;

- on a weekly or bi-weekly basis, where lessons are taught either by the homeroom teacher or an outside trained staff member; and,

- on a periodic basis, where the activities can serve as enrichment.

For maximum results with this program, it is strongly recommended that each Character Builder be focused upon for a minimum of six weeks to two months. Each trait introduces at least five critical skills that not only enhance the trait's acquisition but also students' social and personal competence. *Character Builders* is also most effective when implemented school-wide. The flow sequence for implementing the five core traits for an entire school year would look like this:

Character Builder Monthly Planner

	Sep	Oct	Nov	Dec	Jan	Feb	Mar	Apr	May	Jun
• Responsibility & Trustworthiness	▬▬▬▬	▬▬▬								
• Respect			▬▬▬	▬▬▬						
• Cooperation & Fairness					▬▬▬	▬▬▬				
• Peaceability & Citizenship							▬▬▬	▬▬▬		
• Caring									▬▬▬	▬▬

SCHOOL-WIDE CHARACTER BUILDING

Many schools have found that emphasizing a different Character Builder theme school-wide for a month or six weeks (or more) is a highly successful way for students to acquire these new skills. Focusing at least a month on the same theme allows everyone in the school (staff as well as students) to be aware of the same key concepts. Keep in mind many schools have chosen to implement a Character Builder theme each quarter, some on a semester basis, and a few one each academic year. The time frame should be determined by the desires of the staff. The value of "shared targeting" is powerful. When everyone at the site is reinforcing and modeling the same behavior, students are much more likely to learn a new Character Builder trait and use the skill in their life.

SPECIAL FEATURES OF CHARACTER BUILDERS

The activities in the *Character Builders* series have been developed for students from grade K through 6. As this encompasses a wide range of ages, wherever possible specific ways to adapt the activity for older or younger students are noted. Puppet stories for younger children are in gray tone and accompanied by an image of a puppet. Any activity can be scaled down for younger nonreading/nonwriting students by using pictorial answers or dictating their responses for them. The activity can also easily be converted to a "class meeting" in which responses are reported verbally.

The five manuals in the *Character Builders* series are designed for sequential use. Each manual addresses a distinct character trait and the skills needed to enhance that trait. The manuals are designed to be used as an entire program for a school year (though some schools choose one trait for an entire school year!) Whenever possible, teachers should provide relevant examples of the trait as they materialize in context or in content.

Common to each manual are the following activities:

Character Builder Posters. Each of the five *Character Builders* in this series—Responsibility, Respect, Cooperation, Peaceability and Caring—is illustrated by a poster that can be hung in the classroom (and ideally school walls). The form in the book can be enlarged to a size of at least a 18" × 22". If implementing a school-wide character development program, consider making multiple copies of the posters and then hanging them in dozens of locations, such as the cafeteria, faculty room, halls, restrooms, library, and school office. Place the Character Builder Posters on each teacher's door as well as the doors of the school nurse, secretary, custodians, media specialists and even the school bus driver. The more the Character Builder is accentuated, the greater the likelihood people will "catch the theme." Provide students with a copy of the poster to store in their Character Builder Notebook.

Call Jalmar Press at (800) 662-9662 for a descriptive brochure about *Character Builders* manuals.

Character Builder Notebooks. It is strongly recommended that each student keep a spiral 1/2" notebook to store all completed Character Builder activities. A set of five indexed dividers for each student could separate each of the five core Character Builder traits. A cover for the notebook is found on page RT1c for duplication.

Looks Like/Sounds Like Charts. Each character trait in this series is accompanied by four to five essential skills to teach students. One of the techniques in *Character Builders* used to teach students a new skill is the "looks like/sounds like" chart. Students may then make a copy of the chart on an individual "looks like/sounds like" form provided in the manual and then store it in their Character Builder Notebook. A set of eyes for "Looks Like" and ears for "Sounds Like" are provided on pages RT1f and RT1g to adapt the chart for younger students.

Go/Stop Language. To help students recognize appropriate and inappropriate language and behaviors for each character building theme, an activity called Go/Stop Language—or "stoppers" and "starters"—is included. Go and Stop Signs may easily be converted into stick puppets for role playing with younger children.

Class Meetings. One of the most successful teaching methods in helping students learn the character traits and skills is at the Class Meeting. An explanation of how to use this technique and specific meeting topics are provided in the series. At the conclusion of each meeting, students may write their reflections and thoughts about the topics on the Class Meeting form provided. These forms can be stored in students' Character Builder Notebook.

People need responsibility. They resist assuming it, but they cannot get along without it.
—John Steinbeck

Thought for the Day. Each activity in the series is accompanied by a quote or proverb. A Thought for the Day form is provided to photocopy for students. These thoughts can also be announced over the PA speaker by a student announcer or written each morning on the blackboard. Consider having students copy the thought each day on the form and then store them in their Character Builder Notebooks. This is a great way to integrate the character trait into the literacy curriculum (reading, speaking, writing or listening).

Literature. Each *Character Builders* manual provides dozens of literature selections that can be used to highlight the value of learning the theme. Many teachers use literature as the way to define the trait to students. Choose an appropriate selection and as it is read, ask, "How did the characters demonstrate the Character Builder in the book?" "What effect did their behavior have on the other characters?" or "How did the other characters feel when the character acted . . . " (name the trait).

Vocabulary. To enhance students' language development, vocabulary words synonymous with the character builder terms are provided. Suggested is a key word for each week of the school month followed by a series of synonyms. These words can be used for spelling, vocabulary tests, oral language development, or just fun. These weekly core words are provided on a set of bookmarks that can be duplicated on cardstock or colored paper.

Character Builder Puppets. Each character builder theme—Responsibility, Respect, Cooperation, Peaceability, and Caring—comes with a delightful puppet designed to bring the theme to a concrete level for younger students. The puppet can be duplicated on bright-colored construction paper and attached to a ruler or paper towel tube to instantly liven up these lessons. Puppet stories to make the character traits memorable to young minds accompany some of the activities. A complete description of how to use the puppet is provided in Chapter 1.

Role Models. A natural way to infuse Character Builders into your social studies curriculum is to study real individuals whose lives depict the theme. Each *Character Builders* manual lists several possibilities of current or historical role models who demonstrate the trait. The activity can also serve as a valuable lesson as to the need for the trait.

News Articles. Ask students to collect current news articles of real people demonstating the trait. You might begin each day with a brief review of a real event in the world in which the trait was displayed. Simply take a moment to confirm the trait's value and then hang it in a space devoted to news articles about the targeted trait.

FINAL THOUGHTS

The chains of habit are too weak to be felt until
they are too strong to be broken.
—DR. JOHNSON

Social skills and character traits are most often acquired from watching others do them right. This very premise explains why so many of today's youth are underdeveloped in these traits and skills. With the breakdown of appropriate role models for today's students, it is imperative that educators deliberately exaggerate modeling the character trait and its behaviors at the school site. This is one of the easiest and certainly most important ways to show students the behaviors of character traits and skills. Never forget your own impact on your students. You may well be the only role model a student has to "see" what a Character Builder looks and sounds like.

"Teach a child to choose the right path, and when he is older he will remain upon it."

—The Bible

Dozens of activities and ideas are suggested in this manual as ways for students to practice the skills for each Character Builder trait. Additional practice opportunities are provided by activities in *Esteem Builders: A K-8 Curriculum for Improving Student Achievement, Behavior and School Climate*. And, finally, further activities are offered for parents to reinforce the skills you present in the classroom in *Home Esteem Builders*.

The program is best when it is not a "tack on" new approach but instead infuses the skills and traits into the current curriculum. Before starting a new Character Builder theme, search through your textbooks and book shelves for activities that naturally enhance the theme. Consider subjects such as literature, history, writing, art, science, math, physical education, music . . . every Character Builder has an endless potential of being integrated into your grade-level content. The theme will be not only more manageable for you but more meaningful for your students.

You will notice that while some of your students seem to understand the trait instantly, others need much more repetition and structured practice before they acquire the trait. If you notice some of your students have not grasped the concept, consider a few of these options:

Remodel the Trait. Many students need to "see" the trait and skills again (and again) in order to fully grasp the concept. One, two, or even three times may not be enough. Consider repeating your demonstration lesson with another student and then recreating a new T-chart with students who seem to need additional practice.

Trait Homework. Many teachers involve the parents as partners in character building. Students are required not only to practice the skills and traits at school but also at home. The more practice (particularly in a safe and supportive environment) the greater the likelihood the student will acquire the skill.

"Permanent" Safe Partners. Consider providing students who need additional practice with a "permanent" partner who is not a classmate. The term "permanent" means for a longer duration. The length of such a partnership is up to your discretion but do recognize that students low in security and in social skills are more threatened by demonstrating the trait with a number of different partners. They can benefit from having a "safer" partner they feel more secure with over a longer time period. Safe partners might include a younger student at the school (for example, a student in the sixth grade will find practicing the skill with a second grader or even kindergartener safer than a same-age partner), or a volunteer (a college or high school student or a parent).

Suppose a visitor comes to your site for the first time. He randomly pulls a student aside and asks one question: "What does your teacher or school stand for?" or "What does your teacher think are important kinds of behaviors to do?" Would the student be able to verbalize the Character Builder as an important part of your site? The answer to this question can quickly assess just how successful you've been in teaching Character Builders to your students. If that student can describe the Character Builder, it means you've accentuated the trait well enough that your students can say it to others. Keep on reinforcing it. They'll "own" it soon, which will impact their lives now and forever.

> "You can easily judge the character of a man by how he treats those who can do nothing for him."
>
> —James D. Miles

 **1**

How to Build Character

How to Build Character

The unfortunate thing about this world is that good habits
are so much easier to give up than bad ones.
—W. SOMERSET MAUGHAM

Responsibility is one of the most desirable character traits. It means being accountable, dependable and trustworthy. Once acquired, it nurtures other character traits
such as respect, peaceability, cooperation, and caring. Responsibility is the backbone
of solid citizenship, employability, friendship, and self-reliance. The breakdown of this trait
in our youth should motivate us to do everything we can to rebuild it in our students. Now
here's the good news: responsibility is a trait that can be taught. *Character Builders* shows
you the skills and techniques to ensure that more of our students "catch it."

One of the biggest reasons so many of our students have failed to "catch" a responsible attitude is that the trait seems to be on a decline worldwide. How often have you heard someone say, "Just sue her," or "It's not my fault"? We've become a blame-oriented society quick
with lawsuits and excuses. Keep in mind that one of the easiest ways to "catch" a character
trait is to watch the behavior of someone doing it right. I fear that herein lies one of our
biggest problems: responsibility simply isn't being modeled nearly enough for students to
understand not only its meaning and value but also what it looks and sounds like. If we want
our students to be able to acquire the behaviors of responsibility, then we need to intentionally teach those behaviors. Responsibility is a character trait that extends far beyond the classroom. This trait is vital for success in the home, school, park, neighborhood, workplace, and
nation. This first manual shows you how to help students understand the meaning and value
of personal, as well as social, responsibility so they can do the skills on their own.

Remember, the only place your students may ever see this critical Character Builder demonstrated is by watching you…so intentionally tune up the trait in your behavior and accentuate the value of responsibiliy. It will help your students not only now but in the future.

Educators can aid students in developing the trait of responsibility by taking the following steps:

Steps to Building Student Responsibility

1. Teach the meaning and value of responsibility.
2. Enhance understanding of class rules and responsibilities.
3. Provide practice in the skills of self-control and inner responsibility.
4. Develop learning responsibilities for self and others.

This manual provides practical, research-based activities to teach students this essential Character Builder. The learning outcomes are ones your students will use not only now but for the rest of their lives. Here are some of the lifetime benefits students will acquire from using the lessons in responsibility.

Responsibility Learning Outcomes

- Create a responsible student learning environment that is physically and emotionally safe.

- Develop fair limits to help students know what is expected.

- Establish "meeting rule" expectations for students: a quiet signal, no interrupting, no put downs, and attentive listening.

- Help students recognize what is appropriate responsible behavior.

- Help students acquire the responsibility skill of showing commitment by using a Pledge Shake.

Key Objectives for Responsibility

- Setting up class meetings.
- Making rules.
- Shaking on a pledge.
- Using twelve inch voices.
- Staying calm and in control.
- Apologizing.
- Taking ownership for inappropriate behavior.

- Recognizing choices in behavior.
- Following through.
- Forming Study Buddy partnerships.
- Tracking student progress.
- Modeling responsibility.
- Learning accountability.

RESPONSIBILITY SKILL BUILDERS

Responsibility Theme Poster (RT1a)

Pledge Shake: Gesture of commitment or affirmation (RT14).

Making Rules (RT12).

Calming Down (RT28).

Apologizing (RT31).

Staying Calm (RT27).

> "We need to restore the full meaning of that old word, duty. It is the other side of rights."
>
> —Pearl Buck

Responsibility Vocabulary

Week 1: Responsible

Week 2: Trustworthy

Week 3: Rules

Week 4. Covenant

Models of Responsibility

John Muir	Fredrick Douglas
Albert Schweitzer	John Adams
Susan B. Anthony	James Madison
Colin Powell	Abraham Lincoln
Benjamin Franklin	Harriet Tubman
Caesar Chavez	George Washington
Winston Churchill	Mahatma Ghandi
Jane Adams	Golda Meir
Gloria Steinham	Marie Curie

STEPS TO BUILDING CHARACTER TRAITS

Though each of the five Character Builders in this program are unique and consist of distinct skills and behaviors, the steps to teaching each character trait (Responsibility, Respect, Cooperation, Peaceability, and Caring) are the same. The staff should utilize the same five steps in teaching each Character Builder in this series. Skipping any step will be detrimental to the students' acquisition of the concept. There's an old Chinese proverb which is quite appropriate to the learning process. It says: "If you cut too many corners, you end up going around in circles." Each step is important in helping students learn these five core Character Builders.

RESPONSE + ABILITY

Character Skill Builder Teaching Steps

1. **TARGET:** Focus on the Character Builder for at least 21 days.

2. **DEFINE:** Describe the need, value, and meaning of the trait.

3. **SHOW:** Teach what the trait looks like and sounds like.

4. **DO:** Provide structured practice of the trait for 21 days.

5. **REINFORCE:** Give immediate feedback and encourage use in life.

STEP 1: TARGET

Focus on the Character Builder

The first step to teaching any new character trait, skill or behavior is to target the skill visually (and ideally orally) to students. The more students "see" the trait the more they recognize that "these must be important...there they are again." If Character Builders are being accentuated school-wide, it is important that the poster for each theme and skill be accentuated throughout the school site. Everyone at the school needs to be reminded of the theme.

Quick Ways to Target a Character Builder

- Clearly announce to students what the targeted trait is and keep it posted.

- Keep the Character Builder trait or skill posted as long as possible. Many teachers add a new Character Builder poster to their walls every month or two.

- Tell students your expectations regarding the trait.

- Announce the trait over the loudspeaker or at least start each morning with a one-minute Character Builder announcement.

- If Character Builders are being accentuated school-wide, it is important that the poster for each theme and skill be accentuated throughout the school site. Everyone at the school needs to be reminded of the theme.

Keeping the Focus on Character

There are dozens of ways to focus on character traits and skills. Below are listed some of the simplest as well as some of the most unique ways to accentuate a character trait.

- **Character Builder Poster.** Each Character Builder trait comes with an 8½" × 11" poster. Photocopy the poster on bright-colored paper and hang it on walls for all to see. The form in this book can be enlarged at a printer's to a 18" × 24" size. The Character Builder puppet can be enlarged to hang up as a visual reminder for younger children.

- **Character Builder Assembly.** Many sites implementing school-wide character themes introduce the trait at a school-wide assembly. At this occasion the staff describes why the trait is important, distributes the poster to students, and even presents a short skit or movie about the trait.

- **Screen Saver.** This one wins the prize for the "most unique way to accentuate a character trait." I saw it at a magnet school in computers and technology. Each day a staff or student member wrote a brief sentence describing a school rule, theme or learning message about the targeted Character Builder on the site's central screen saver. Whenever anyone at the school used a computer, the first thing they saw was the screen saver message accentuating the trait.

- **Campaign Posters.** Student-made posters are often the simplest way to accentuate a character trait. Students can draw the guidelines using material such as colored poster board, marking pens, and construction paper. Posters can also be computer-generated and printed on colored paper. However posters are made, be sure to hang them everywhere and anywhere on school and classroom walls.

- **Flag Pole Banner.** On visiting a middle school in Austin, Texas, I knew when I was in the parking lot what behaviors that staff was accentuating for their students. A banner made from an old white sheet hung on the flag pole. Imprinted with bold-colored permanent marking, the banner stated one word: "EFFORT!" Each month the staff selected a different trait, and a group of students volunteered to make and hang the banner.

- **Character Builder Announcements.** By using the school loud speaker system, students can be orally reminded of the character traits and skills. Many schools use the first and last minute of each school day for Character Builder reminders. Principals can announce names of students "caught demonstrating the trait." Students can describe ways to appropriately demonstrate the traits or behaviors.

- **Character Builder Theme Songs.** A unique way to accentuate each Character Builder is by selecting a "theme song" to match each character trait. Play it over the loud speaker before the bell rings and during lunch. For example, the song from the television show, "Cheers," is a great way to accentuate the theme of Cooperation. There is no better song for the theme of Respect than Aretha Franklin's tune by the same name, "Respect."

> "Few things help an individual more than to place responsibility upon him, and to let him know that you trust him."
>
> —Booker T. Washington

STEP 2: DEFINE

Describe the Need, Value and Meaning of the Trait

The second step to teaching a new character trait or behavior is to convey to students exactly what the trait means and why it is important to learn. Though the trait may be targeted in the classroom and on dozens of posters throughout the campus, never assume students understand what the trait means. The trait should always be explained to students so that they can understand the concept within their knowledge base and experience. Though each Character Builder poster has a carefully constructed definition, keep in mind a definition generated by the students will be even more powerful. Here are a few other ways to define new traits and behaviors to students.

Quick Ways to Define a Character Builder

- Tell students specifically why they should learn the skill.

- Clearly explain the value of learning the trait.

- Specifically define the trait to students. "This is what I mean when I say the word caring…."

- Keep the definition posted in your classroom and, ideally, all around the school.

- Use your own personal examples to make the definition concrete.

- Find literature selections that define the trait.

- Ask students to clip news articles of events or people demonstrating the theme.

Below are many powerful suggestions of specific ways you can define a Character Builder for your students:

- **Define in Teachable Moments.** Use teachable moments to accentuate, define and model new behaviors to students. You might accentuate the behavior of "encouragement" by patting a student on the back and saying: "Keep it up. I know you can do it!" Take one more second to label and define the trait by saying, "Did you notice I just encouraged you?" Finally, define the behavior to the student in context by adding…"because I just patted you on the back and told you I knew you could do it." Many students need a moment to process the concept in context.

- **Label Traits as Students Use Them.** Whenever you see or hear a student displaying the targeted trait, take a moment to label it to the rest of the students. Point out specifically what the student did that demonstrated the trait and remember to be consistent in the use of terms. For instance, if "respect" is the term that appears on the Character Builder poster, use this same term to reinforce a student's behavior. Here are the steps to labeling a new behavior.

  1. *First, point out the behavior as soon as convenient with a label.*

     It is always best to point out the behavior the moment it happens so the student will be more likely to recall what he or she did. Also, any other students who are near the reinforced student will also benefit from hearing "what was done right." Suppose you are reinforcing "respect." Stop and label the appropriate behavior to the student:

     "Alex, that was respectful…"

> "It is not fair to ask of others what you are not willing to do yourself."
>
> —Eleanor Roosevelt

2. *Second, tell the student specifically what they did that was appropriate.*

Usually, you can begin with the word "because" and then confirm to the student exactly what he or she did that was "respectful."

"...because you waited until I was finished
talking before you spoke."

- **Tell the Trait's Benefits.** Skills and behaviors are more meaningful and relevant to students if they understand the benefit of learning the skill. Take a moment to say the name of the Character Builder or the skill and why it's important. For example, "This month we will be learning about the value of caring. It's such an important trait because it helps make the world a kinder and gentler place."

- **Share Personal Beliefs.** Students need to hear your convictions regarding the trait. Why do you personally feel the trait is important? If you are targeting the trait of "respect," you might tell students how adamant you feel about not talking negatively about yourself or others. For instance, you could say: "One of the things that bothers me most is when I hear someone saying something unkind about themselves or someone else. I know unkindness hurts. In this classroom it is not allowed." Show them with your own behavior how strongly you believe in what you say.

- **Student Reporters.** One of the easiest ways to demonstrate the need for the trait is to point out its value in context. Anytime someone displays the trait, take a moment to label the Character Builder to students. Suppose you are accentuating "caring." Ask students to begin looking for others demonstrating the trait at the school. These students can assume the role of "reporters." Their job is to report back to the class who demonstrated the trait, what the student did, and most important, the effect the student's actions had on another individual. The sequence might sound like this:

TEACHER: Did anyone see someone who was caring today?

JOHN: I did. I saw Jennifer being caring.

TEACHER: What did you see Jennifer do that was caring?

JOHN: I saw her help another student who fell down. She went to the nurse's office to get a Band-Aid and get help.

TEACHER: That was caring. Did you notice how the hurt student felt after Jennifer helped her?

JOHN: Well, at first the student was crying really hard. Jennifer kept talking quietly to her and pretty soon the girl stopped crying.

TEACHER: How do you think the girl felt when Jennifer showed she cared about her?

JOHN: I think she felt better inside.

"No snowflake in an avalanche ever feels respon- sible."

—Stanislaw Jersy Lee

The dialogue between the teacher and John may have taken no more than a minute, but it was a powerful exchange. The teacher verified not only to John but also to the other students the kind of positive effect caring can have on others. The simple conversation became a significant lesson highlighting the need for learning caring.

STEP 3: SHOW
Teach What the Trait Looks Like and Sounds Like

Now comes the moment when you teach the Character Builder to your students. Very often the prior steps (targeting and defining) are skipped. As a result, many students fail to learn the skills so critical to the trait. There is no perfect way to teach the trait. A few suggested techniques that have been field-tested and proven successful are offered. The most important part of effective teaching is to try and make the trait as "hands on" and meaningful as possible. Never assume students have the language or cognitive acquisition of the trait. Many do not. You can make a significant difference in your students' lives (both now and in the future!) by modeling the trait yourself and making your Character Builder lessons as concrete as possible.

Quick Ways to Show a Character Builder

- Model the trait showing specific behaviors.

- Another staff member can model the trait with you to the class in a quick role play.

- Send a videocamera crew of students on a search for other students modeling the trait. Capture the Character Builder trait on video and then play it for everyone else to see.

- Create, with students, a T-Chart of the skill/trait and, as you develop the chart, model what it looks like and sounds like.

- Identify famous individuals who emulate the skill/trait. Ask students to read biographies about their lives and/or report what the individual specifically did to demonstrate the skill.

- Photograph students demonstrating the trait and make a chart students can refer to.

Role Playing

One of the best ways to teach behaviors or traits is by role playing what it looks like to students. This need not take more than 30 seconds (honestly!), but it is a step that should not be skipped. Your students need to know exactly what the trait looks and sounds like. Role playing can be adapted for younger children by having them play out Character Builder behaviors using the puppets. Suppose you want to teach students the behavior of attentive listening. Here are the steps you could use to model the trait.

1. Begin by choosing a confident student or another staff member to help you role play the trait. The two of you should stand in a location so that all of your students can see your behavior (the other person in the role play is not who the students are to watch—it's you!) Tell students: "In the next minute you'll have the opportunity to watch what listening looks and sounds like. Watch me carefully. I'm going to show (name of the other person) that I'm listening to her."

2. Tell the other person to relax and think of anything he did before coming to school that day that he would like to share. Explain that he can say anything and that if he runs out of things to say he is allowed to make things up. You might have another student time you so that the activity does not extend beyond 30 seconds.

3. As the other person begins talking, your role is to demonstrate to the group what the Character Builder skill (in this instance, "attentive listening") looks like. Turn the participant towards you so that the two of you are standing face to face and sideways to the group so that the class sees only your outside shoulders. Once the student begins speaking, deliberately don't say anything except "uh huh" or "yes." Your job is to convey good listening behaviors such as facing your partner squarely at all times, not interrupting, raising your eyebrows at key points, smiling and nodding, appearing animated or enthused, leaning forward slightly, looking directly into the speaker's eyes, and keeping your arms at your sides. At the end of the minute, thank the participant and tell the class to give the person a big hand.

4. On the blackboard, transparency or chart paper draw a large T-chart that covers the full space of the medium you are working with. Write the name of the Character Builder trait or skill at the top of the board. To the left, write "Looks Like" and to the right side "Sounds Like." Now create a T-Chart such as the one below:

Attentive Listening

 Looks Like   **Sounds Like**

5. Tell students you just showed them what the skill of "attentive listening" looks and sounds like. Now ask them to specify what they saw you do that showed them you were attentively listening to the participant. Remind students of the rules for brainstorming. You may want to post the Brainstorming Rules Poster (RT13a) near the chart to remind students of the rules. Emphasize that "no put downs are allowed."

6. For younger students, images of an eye for "Looks Like" and an ear for "Sounds Like" are included in each manual to duplicate, cut out and tape to the T-chart. Say, "Remember, I want you to tell me first only what you saw me do. What you saw me do is called 'Looks Like.'" List the group's ideas under the "Looks Like" side of the chart. Continually remind the group to be very specific. Write the concrete list of words or phrases students generate in the discussion. If students have difficulty recalling listening behaviors, you might wish to remind them by remodeling the behavior with your body. For example, to help students recall that your body was facing square to the student, you might ask: "Where was my body facing? Where were my shoulders? Were they here (turn your shoulders away from the student) or were they here?" (Turn your shoulders square to the student.) When a list has been obtained, ask the group to now refer to the "Sounds Like" side of the chart.

A completed group chart might look like this:

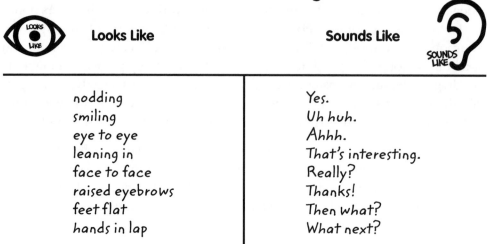

Attentive Listening

Looks Like	Sounds Like
nodding	Yes.
smiling	Uh huh.
eye to eye	Ahhh.
leaning in	That's interesting.
face to face	Really?
raised eyebrows	Thanks!
feet flat	Then what?
hands in lap	What next?

7. Emphasize to the students that you deliberately did not say much during the activity other than "uh huh" and "yes." The first step to attentive listening is making sure your body is sending messages that show you are listening.

8. Mention that the kinds of things we can say to demonstrate we are listening can be taught at a later time and will be added to the list. You might ask the group for a few phrases or words a student could say to another student to let the person know he or she is listening. These could be included under "Sounds Like," such as: "Yes," "That's interesting," "Really?," "I didn't know that," "Thanks!," "Then what?" and "What next?"

It is important to create a T-chart of behaviors for each Character Builder trait you teach to students, and it is always more meaningful for students to create their own charts rather than be provided with one "pre-made." A T-chart form in Character Builders is provided for students to fill out and keep in their Character Builder Notebooks following each lesson.

The completed T-chart should then be hung in the classroom as a visual reminder of the trait or the behavior. New words and behaviors should continue to be added to the chart throughout the year as students recognize additional Character Building behaviors.

Chart Variations for Younger Students

• **Photographs.** Capture students actually displaying the Character Builder behaviors on film. Develop the pictures, enlarge them slightly on a copying machine and paste them on a chart labeling the trait.

"Make it a point to do something every day that you don't want to do. This is the golden rule for acquiring the habit of doing your duty without pain."

—Mark Twain

- **Butcher Paper.** Ask a student to lay down on a piece of long butcher paper and trace around their body outline. Hang up the paper and ask students to now show what different parts of the body do to show the speaker the Character Builder trait. Print these behaviors inside the outline next to the body part. For "listening," for instance, a chart might include: mouth closed, hands in lap, feet flat on the floor, head nodding, eyes on speaker.

STEP 4: DO

Provide Structured Practice of the Trait

Showing students what the Character Builder looks and sounds like is not enough. In most cases, students must be provided with frequent structured opportunities to practice the new behaviors. In fact, behavior management theory tells us it generally takes 21 days of repetition or practice before a new behavior is acquired. This is an important rule to keep in mind as you try these activities with your students. You will see change if you continue to model the behavior, provide consistent opportunities for students to practice the skill, and reinforce appropriate behaviors. One of the greatest benefits of Character Builders is the program is designed to be used for a minimum of 21 days.

Quick Ways to Practice a Character Builder

- Allow students at least 21 days to practice the skill in frequent structured opportunities.
- Practice sessions can be done in "learning buddies" or "base teams."
- Role play the skill/trait. Younger students can role play Character Builder behaviors using the puppet.
- Students can keep a "reflection log" of their behavior progress with the trait.
- Use any teachable moments to ask, "Is that a stopper or a starter?"
- Character Builder "homework" can be assigned by requiring students to practice the skill at home with their family.

STEP 5: REINFORCE

Give Immediate Feedback and Encourage Use in Life

The final step to teaching a Character Builder is to reinforce students' appropriate behavior or correct inappropriate behavior as soon as it is convenient to do so and encourage them to use the trait in their own lives. There are two important reasons to reinforce the Character Builder trait or skill:

1. It helps clarify to the student that he/she is on the right track and that he/she should keep up the good work. The student immediately recognizes the demonstrated trait because you pointed it out on the spot. Behavior management theory says the student is more likely to repeat the behavior again because he knows what he did right.

2. The reinforced student serves as a model to any other students who happened to be nearby the moment the student was recognized. Keep in mind most social skills are learned through watching others. The frustrating part of teaching for many educators has been the simple fact that appropriate role models are breaking down for our students. Anytime we can use a peer as an appropriate role model and specifically let other students know what the student did that was correct, we are helping those students learn the appropriate behavior.

Quick Ways to Reinforce a Character Builder

- Give specific feedback ASAP: students did the trait right or wrong.

- Tell students exactly what they did right or wrong. If they were correct, say what they did right. If the behavior was wrong, say what they can do next time. Waiting until the end of the day is too late. With some kids, waiting five minutes later is too late. Students benefit from immediate correction.

- Redo the behavior with students on the spot by pointing out or showing exactly what the students should do to replace the incorrect behavior pattern.

- Give students "constructive criticism." Tell what was wrong. Tell what to do to make it right. Be brief. Be private. Be specific and remember: emphasize only the student's behavior, never their character.

- Reinforce to students whenever the skill is done correctly. Use "catching the skill done correctly" as a teachable moment for the rest of the class.

- Provide students with reinforcement tickets, coupons and awards. Character Builders includes a number of these forms for each character trait and skill.

- The Character Builder puppet for each trait can be constantly used as a reinforcer for children. Look for a child who has correctly demonstrated the Character Builder and quietly place the puppet on his/her desk. This child then looks for another student demonstrating the trait and places the puppet on this person's desk. It's a silent reinforcer that tunes students into looking for appropriate behaviors.

STUDENT CHARACTER BUILDERS

One can acquire everything in solitude—except character.
—HENRI BEYLE

Students can be instrumental in helping peers (and staff) "catch a character attitude" by involving them in the planning and implementation of the Character Builder activities. Ideally, these students should be of various ages. This committee can become a core group of students for the year or can be changed monthly. If the committee is to be a school-wide group of students, one or two faculty members can become committee advisors whose job is to coordinate the student group. Possibilities for involving students are endless. Here are a few ideas other school sites have used:

"Duty is the sublimest word in the language; you can never do more than your duty; you should never wish to do less."
—Robert E. Lee

- **Student Campaign Committee.** As each new Character Builder is introduced, the Student Campaign Committee begins a blitz of creating banners, signs and posters to hang up around the school convincing the rest of the students of the merit of the theme.

- **Student Announcement Group.** Many classrooms, as well as schools, begin the day with a one-minute message "advertising" the theme. The advertisement may include a powerful quotation to think about, an announcement reinforcing students "caught" demonstrating the Character Builder or even a quick commercial stating the value of learning the theme. Teachers ask different students daily or weekly to assume this role. Administrators have students make announcements over the school PA system.

- **Skit Committee.** This group of students creates a skit or role play about the Character Builder and performs it at either a school-wide assembly or in each classroom. The skit shows other students the value of the trait as well as what the Character Builder looks and sounds like. (Idea from Lakeview School, Minneapolis.)

- **Video Crew.** If you have access to video equipment, you might consider teaching a core group of students how to use it. A student video crew could record actual students demonstrating the trait. They might also video the students' Character Builder skit. The video is then shown in each classroom.

HOW TO USE CHARACTER BUILDER PUPPETS

Developmental learning theory clearly tells us that young children learn best through concrete experiences. The Character Builder puppets in this series were designed with this concept in mind. Each book is accompanied by a puppet as well as stories, role playing and follow-up activities that present the core lessons in a meaningful and fun way.

Meet the Character Builder Puppets

Responsibility

Able

Behavior Traits: He's a star you can always count on; he's dependable, trustworthy, reliable.

RP1

Caring

Sunshine

Behavior Traits: She's a sun who brings warmth and happiness to those she touches.

RP5

Respect

Admiral

Behavior Traits: He's a moon you can look up to and admire; he's earned respect through caring actions.

RP4

Disrespect/Negativity

Stinger

Behavior Traits: He's an unhappy star who puts others down.

RP3

Cooperation

Pal and Goldie

Behavior Traits: They are planets who depend on each other; they work together to accomplish their goals.

RP6

Irresponsible

Spinner

Behavior Traits: He's a comet who has poor judgment and a quick temper; he spins out of control.

RP7

Peaceableness

Sparky

Behavior Traits: He's a star who is always positive; he sparkles and shines with builder-uppers.

RP2

Aggressive

Burner

Behavior Traits: He's a meteor who is belligerent and attacking; he burns himself out.

RP8

Note: Larger versions of the above characters can be found in the Puppets section.

The Character Builder puppets will appear periodically in each book to reinforce a lesson or concept. If they are to be used in the activity, they will be listed in the materials section. Just look for the gray tone and a small replica of the puppet. A story for younger children using the puppet to describe the Character Builder concepts is then provided.

There are many ways the puppet can be used to liven up the session and reinforce the Character Builder concepts. Here are a few ways the puppet images can be used to make the lessons concrete and memorable for young children:

- *Felt Puppet.* To make the puppet durable for years of use, trace and cut the puppet head shape provided in each manual onto felt. Glue the felt shape onto heavy cardboard and cut it out again for a stiff figure. Three dimensional features can be attached to the figure with a glue gun: buttons, movable eyes, yarn hair, pom-poms, and even sequins or rickrack. Finally, attach a wooden dowel to the back of the puppet with heavy masking tape or a glue gun to create a puppet ready to tell character building stories.

- *Paper Stick Puppet.* The easiest way to make any of the Character Builder puppets is simply to duplicate the puppet head provided in the manual onto colored construction paper or cardstock-weight paper. Cut out the shape and tape it to a paper towel tube, a ruler, or a wooden dowel. Students love making their own puppets with you.

- *Paper Bag Puppet.* Duplicate the puppet head onto colored construction paper or cardstock-weight paper, cut out the shape and glue it to the front flap of a lunch-size paper bag. Features can be added to the face or body using items such as colored paper scraps, noodles, egg carton pieces, pipe cleaners, wall paper samples, yarn, bric-a-brac, and fabric.

- *Shape Book Cover.* Duplicate the puppet shape onto light-colored construction paper or cardstock. Cut two copies along the outside margin of the shape for a front and back book cover along with several pieces of writing paper so that the cover and writing paper are the same size. Place the writing pages inside the front and back cover and staple the pages along the top or sides. The book may now be used by students to write, draw, dictate further adventure stories about the characters, or describe what they learned in the lesson.

- *Award.* Duplicate the puppet head on cardstock or light-colored construction paper and cut out the shape. Punch two holes along the top, string a long 36" piece of yarn through the holes and tie the ends into a knot. The shape can be hung from the neck of any student who demonstrates the Character Builder trait or behavior.

- *Hats.* Fun hats for students to wear while role playing the stories are easy to make. Here are two quick versions:

  1. Fold up the opening on a medium-size grocery bag about two inches. Duplicate a copy of the shape on colored construction paper or cardstock, cut it out and glue or staple it to the front. The student puts the bag on his head for a hat.

  2. Duplicate a copy of the puppet shape on colored construction paper or cardstock and cut it out. Cut a strip of tagboard or construction paper 3" × 28", bring the ends together so they overlap about two inches and staple them. Finally staple the puppet head shape to the front of the strip to wear as a hat.

- *Puppet Bag.* Copy the puppet head shape onto paper and cut it out along the outside edge. Glue or staple the head to the front of a lunch-size brown bag. The opened bag sits on top of students' desks. Use the puppet bags to send notes of encouragement (from you and the students) or to congratulate one another on demonstrating the character trait symbolized by the puppet.

- *Starter and Stopper Puppets.* To help students reflect on appropriate and inappropriate language and behaviors for each of the Character Builder traits, two traffic shapes are included for role playing and storytelling. The Go Sign (page RT2d) signifies "starter" language and behaviors, or the kinds of things people who demonstrate the character trait would say and do. The Stop Sign (page RT2e) represents "stopper" language and behaviors or inappropriate words and actions that do not depict the character trait. The stopper sign is duplicated on red construction paper or cardstock and cut out; the starter sign on green. The signs can easily be made into puppets by gluing, taping or stapling a paper towel tube, ruler or wooden dowel to the back of the shape. The stick is now ready for role playing. The shapes can also be glued to charts, pinned to bulletin boards or taped on a blackboard to enhance a lesson using the concept.

> "In times like the present, men should utter nothing for which they would not willingly be responsible through time and in eternity."
>
> —Abraham Lincoln

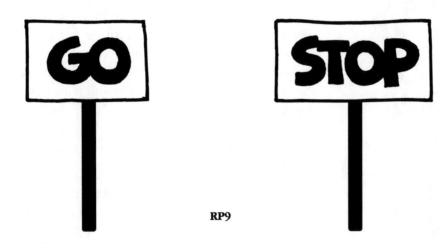

RP9

- *Looks Like/Sounds Like Puppets.* To help students recognize the kinds of things people who demonstrate the character trait say and do, two shapes—an ear and an eye—are included in the manual. The ear and eye shapes are duplicated on construction paper and cut out. The shapes can then be glued, taped or stapled to a paper towel tube, ruler or wooden dowel for a stick puppet to use in role playing. The shapes can also be glued to charts, pinned to bulletin boards or taped on a blackboard to enhance a lesson using the concept.

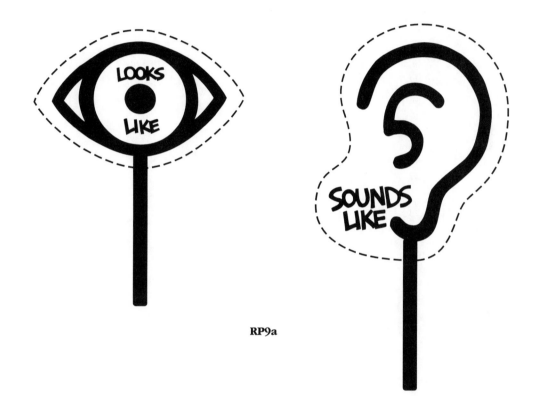

RP9a

The concrete activities provided in this manual as well as the other four supporting books in this series offer endless possibilities for building the essential character traits in your students. Remember, to help students learn these new skills for now, as well as for the rest of their lives, keep the five steps to enhancing Character Builder skills in mind:

RESPONSE + ABILITY

1. **TARGET:** Focus on the Character Builder for at least 21 days.

2. **DEFINE:** Describe the need, value and meaning of the trait.

3. **SHOW:** Teach what the trait looks like and sounds like.

4. **DO:** Provide structured practice of the trait for 21 days.

5. **REINFORCE:** Give immediate feedback and encourage use in life.

2

Teaching Responsibility

RESPONSIBILITY

- Response + Ability: Doing What is Right; Being Answerable and Accountable to Yourself and Others

CHARACTER BUILDER STEP #1:

- Teach the Meaning and Value of Responsibility

2

Teaching Responsibility

Responsible persons are mature people who have taken charge of themselves and their conduct, who own their actions and own up to them—who answer for them. We help foster a mature sense of responsibility in our children in the same way that we help cultivate their other desirable traits: by practice and by example.

—WILLIAM BENNETT

Responsibility is not something you give to a child. They must learn it and earn it themselves. Educators do have incredible power to create the conditions in a classroom and school site that nurture and support the acquisition of this critical Character Builder. Self-responsibility is indispensable to positive self-esteem and self-reliance. The first step toward the acquisition of self-responsibility is creating an environment that allows the enhancement of self-reliance and also helps children learn what it means to be accountable. International authority on self-esteem, Dr. Nathaniel Branden, says it best:

> "The abandonment of personal accountability makes self-esteem, as well as decent and benevolent social relationships, impossible. In its worst manifestation, it becomes a license to kill. If we are to have a world that works, we need a culture of accountability."

CHARACTER BUILDER STEP #1

Teach the Meaning and Value of Responsibility

Few things help an individual more than to place responsibility upon him, and to let him know that you trust him.

—BOOKER T. WASHINGTON

This first group of Character Building activities is designed to help students understand the meaning and value of the trait, "responsibility." Too often we assume students have an awareness of responsibility, but such an assumption greatly hinders their acquisition of the trait. Remember, the more students understand why the trait or skill is valuable, the more motivated they will be to practice the skill until they "own" it and use it for life.

WHAT IS RESPONSIBILITY?   RT 1

Purpose: To help students understand the meaning of the trait, responsibility; to teach students the T-chart concept of what the theme of responsibility "looks like" and "sounds like."

Thought: *You can't escape the responsibility of tomorrow by evading it today.*—Abraham Lincoln

Vocabulary: Taking ownership, having control over yourself, being accountable, acting dependably, doing what is right.

Materials:

- Responsibility Poster (RT1a); one per student and one enlarged poster size.

- Character Builder Notebook Cover; one per student (RT1c).

For older students:
- Looks Like/Sounds Like (RT1d).

For younger students:
- Eye/Ear/Heart Images (RT1f, RT1g and RT1h); duplicate on construction paper. Cut out the patterns and use double stick tape to attach to the blackboard.

- Able the Shooting Star Puppet (RT1b).

- How I Feel (RT1e).

Procedure: To create the hand puppet for younger students: Cut out two identical puppet shapes from the original pattern. Ideally, you want to cut the shapes out of heavy, non-fraying fabric such as felt. Hand or machine stitch the two shapes together ¼" from the edges, leaving at least 6" open at the bottom for a hand to fit through. The material can also be attached using a glue gun.

A less durable hand puppet can be made from two pieces of heavy paper, though it will be difficult to bend the shape when the puppet is acting in the scenes. When using material other than felt, cut the puppet at least ½" larger than the original pattern. Turn the two pieces right sides facing together and then machine or hand stitch ¼" from the outside edge.

Now turn the two sewn pieces cut from material or heavy paper inside out. The puppet is now ready to be decorated with movable eyes, yarn hair, a yarn or felt mouth, or any other features of your choice.

To begin the activity, write the term "responsibility" on a chart or the board and ask for meanings from students. Responses might include, taking ownership, having control over yourself, being accountable, acting dependably, doing what is right.

Introduce the first theme poster: Responsibility (RT1a). Define the term "responsibility" as, "doing what is right; being answerable and accountable to yourself and others." Explain that for the first few weeks of school, students will be learning what responsibility is and why this trait is important to help them succeed. Tell them they will also learn how the trait of responsibility helped form our country, and they will have a chance to set a few rules for the class.

To make the idea of responsibility concrete, you could tell students a story. Say: "Responsibility is like a star and, like a star in the night sky, someone who is responsible is always constant and dependable. When you get lost, a responsible person can be counted on to guide you in the right direction. He is capable of following through successfully on what he is expected to do.

"A star's job is to shine at night while the sun brings daylight to the other side of the world. It never says it's too tired and doesn't feel like shining tonight. And it doesn't burn out halfway through the night and go to sleep on the job. A star is there even when we can't see it. During the day, the sun shines so brightly that we can't see the star shine. But that doesn't stop it from shining. It carries out its duties even when no one is looking."

Able the Responsible Star

For younger students, introduce Able the Shooting Star Puppet. Then tell them a story: "Able is the name of a shooting star who had done his job well for many, many thousands of years. But one day he felt as if everyone was taking him for granted. 'Why should I keep shining and shooting when no one seems to notice me for more than a second or two?' he thought. 'Everyone is sleeping at night. They won't know whether I'm shooting across the sky or not.'

"So Able planned to party around the clock. He invited dozens of star buddies, to help him celebrate his nights off. He bought lots of cakes and cookies, blew up balloons to string across the sky, and planned games like ice hockey and skiing. One of his friends offered to bring the CD's and another shooting star said he would streak from one galaxy to the next to personally escort everyone to the party.

"At the party Able was having the time of his life. He and his friends ate nothing but desserts because that's all anyone wanted to eat. When his guests ran out of cakes and cookies, they plucked clouds out of the night sky and ate them like marshmallows. The music blared so loudly that no one could hear what anyone else said, but no one seemed to mind because they were having too much fun skiing. With the mellow warmth from the stars shut down, the temperature was ideal for winter games.

"Meanwhile, a little boy on planet earth had gotten lost in the woods behind his house. He had walked this path many times before and thought he knew his way home. But last night the sky went pitch black and the weather suddenly changed from a cool spring breeze to a bone chilling wind that dug like icicles through the sleeves of his thin shirt. The little boy tried to gather some leaves around him to keep warm but the wind kept blowing them away. Too exhausted to chase after leaves any longer, the boy curled up under a tree and fell asleep, hoping the stars would come out soon so he could find his way home.

"Hours later when he awoke, the sky was even darker and the ground even colder than before. It was so dark that the boy couldn't see his hand in front of his face. Not even a shooting star passed by to take away the terror of the darkness. Too frightened to wander around in the dark, he began shouting for help. Maybe a passerby with a flashlight would hear him. But no humans could hear his cry because they were staying inside to avoid the bad weather. Able was on his fifteenth trip to gather marshmallow clouds for his guests when he was surprised to hear what sounded like someone in distress. He shot closer to the earth and turned on his light to see who was making all the noise.

"The little boy fell back and shielded his eyes from the star's brightness. 'Who are you?' the boy asked. 'I'm Able the Shooting STAR. STAR stands for Success Through Acting Responsibly. I'm Able to show you the way out of here,' he replied confidently. The boy couldn't believe what he was hearing. 'I wouldn't be out here in the first place if it hadn't been for you,' he fumed. 'Where were you and the other stars last night? I depend on you to find my way home. I could have frozen to death.'

When Able saw how cold the boy was he turned up the heat on his star button. In minutes, the natural color returned to his white lips and blue fingertips. Then Able shined his brightest light on the foot path until the boy got out of the woods and ran into his house. The shooting star felt satisfied because he had taken care of his responsibilities.

"Able returned to the party to find many of his friends sick to their stomachs from eating too many desserts. Others were arguing about who should get up and turn down the volume on the music. Able turned off the music and with all his friends gathered in one place, he told them, 'I believed that people were taking us for granted and that if we didn't do what we're supposed to do no one would care. But I was wrong. Tonight I realized that others are depending on us to do our jobs. We are responsible for creating a safe and warm environment and for guiding others on the path that will lead them to success.' When Able had finished speaking, the stars began leaving one by one to go back to their places in the sky. Able spent the rest of his life shooting across the sky so that others could catch a star to success."

CHAPTER TWO
Teaching Responsibility

Brainstorm with students what responsibility "looks like" and "sounds like." List their responses on the T-chart. Introduce the third element "feels like" by asking students, "How does responsibility feel?" Ask students to write down their personal responses on the How I Feel form. For younger students, use the eye and ear shapes in place of the words "looks like" and "sounds like." Tape up the heart shape when discussing how responsibility feels.

Follow-up Activities: Provide students with a copy of the Responsibility Poster. Ask them to color the poster and put the completed form inside their Character Builder Notebook. Younger students can also make their own Able Puppet to take home and play with.

The Behavior of Responsibility

 Sounds Like

Looks Like

Sounds Like	Looks Like
"I am responsible for myself!" "I know the rules!" "You can count on me." "I accept the consequence. I know I was wrong." "This is unacceptable." "I'm sorry. It was my error." "I can control my behavior." "I use a calm voice." "I know what behavior is expected of me." "It is my job to keep the boards clean." "I'll be responsible for taking care of the class pet." "Trust me, I'll bring the book back." "I promise I'll turn in the paper tomorrow." "You know I'll finish my reading on time. I always do." "I have a big project due. I'm going to start right now." "I always do my homework before I watch TV. That way I know I'll get it done." "My team members can always count on me to do what I say I will."	Being on time. Not interrupting. Turning in homework. Listening attentively. Speaking in a calm voice. Speaking in turn. Freezing when you see the hand signal.

GO/STOP RESPONSIBILITY LANGUAGE

RT 2

Purpose: To help students understand the meaning of the trait, responsibility.

Thought: *A new position of responsibility will usually show a man to be a far stronger creature than was supposed.*—William James

Literature: *Responsibility* by Elain P. Goley (Rourke Enterprises, 1989). Pictures and a simple text make this the perfect book to teach the trait of responsibility to young children.

Materials:

- Character Builder Notebooks (RT1c).

- Chalk and blackboard, or chart paper and felt pens.

For older students:
- Looks Like/Sounds Like form (RT1d); one per student.

- Starter and Stopper form (RT2a).

For younger or non-reading students:
- Responsibility Pictures (RT2b) and Irresponsibility Pictures (RT2c); one copy of each enlarged slightly on a copy machine.

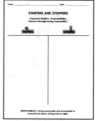

RT2a

RT2b

- Stopper and Starter Images (RT2d and RT2e); duplicated on red and green paper construction paper respectively; attach with masking tape to a ruler, paper towel tube, or dowel.

- Able the Shooting Star Puppet (RT1b).

RT2c

Note: To adapt this activity for younger or non-writing students, enlarge the pictures on Responsibility Pictures and Irresponsibility Pictures slightly on a copying machine. Cut out the individual pictures and use them for the T-chart activity in place of words. The Stoppers and Starters can be made into signs by attaching them with masking tape to a ruler, paper towel tube, or dowel. Consider using the Able Character Builder Puppet to role play these concepts with students.

RT1b

RT2d

Procedure: Begin by creating a T-chart. On the blackboard or on large chart paper write the word "Responsibility." Make a large "T" shape under the word. On the left of the "T" write the term "Sounds Like" and to the right of the "T" write "Doesn't Sound Like." Tape the green "starter" sign above the "Sounds Like" section and the red "stopper" sign above "Doesn't Sound Like." Explain that the green "Sounds Like" column are things that responsible people say. The Go Sign stands for "starter" language, the kinds of things to remember to say because they will help students succeed. The column on the right is for "stoppers," the kinds of statements people who are not responsible would say. For younger students, tape the starter and stopper signs to the chart.

RT2e

To get younger students thinking about what GO and STOP language sounds like, use the puppet to give examples of what the Able Character Builder Puppet would say. For instance, GO statements might include: "My light will guide you to success," "I am successful because I act responsibly," "I back up my words with actions," "I will always be there for you," and "Catch a star to success." STOP statements might include: "Everyone takes me for granted" and "Nobody cares if I shine or not."

Review the term "responsibility" and ask students to think of times they or someone they were with acted responsibly. You might need to provide a few examples: Sally broke the neighbor's window and offered to pay for it; Johnny turned his assignment in on time; Monica apologized to Mary for breaking a confidence; Julie felt like she was losing control and walked away to calm down; Ruben saw Bill was hurt and went to get help. Remind students that acting responsibly is doing what is right for themselves and others.

Ask students to think of statements a responsible person might say. Write these ideas under the "starters" section. If students have a difficult time generating comments, go back to the examples given above. What might Ruben say when Bill gets hurt?

After a few examples, move to the right side under the STOP section and ask students to think of statements someone who was not acting responsibly might say. Write these examples on the board.

Leave the chart on the wall so additional comments from students can be added under the GO side as they occur in the classroom. Students will begin to focus on responsible actions and statements as the trait is accentuated.

Follow-up Activity: Students can complete their own T-chart (RT2a) for their Character Builder Notebook.

RT2a

RESPONSIBILITY

Sounds Like	Does Not Sound Like

"My project is due tomorrow."
"I can do better."
"I will do it."
"I will try my best."
"I know the rules."
"This is acceptable."
"This is unacceptable."
"The correct answer is..."
"I'm following the rules."
Calm and friendly voice.
"I know what behavior is
    expected of me."
"Thank you."
"Please."
"I will use a calm voice and
    stay in control."
	"I can't remember when my
	    project is due."
	"I won't do it."
	"Oh well, why bother?"
	"I don't understand."
	"I can't do any better."
	"It's close enough."
	"I give up."
	"It wasn't worth it."
	"Somebody else will do it."
	"I don't think I can do it."
	"Let's just quit."
	"I don't know what he wants
	    me to do."

CALENDAR OF RESPONSIBILITY   RT 3

Purpose: To reinforce the Character Builder of responsibility on a daily basis for a month.

Materials: Calendar of Responsibility (RT3); one per student.

Thought: *No man was ever endowed with a right without being at the same time saddled with a responsibility.*—Gerald W. Johnson

RT3

Procedure: Have students put a copy of the Calendar of Responsibility in their notebook. Explain that students are assigned one activity from the calendar each day of the month. The activity should be written in their theme notebook. Students can quickly pair up and share the results of their responsibility homework assignment with their study buddies.

RESPONSIBILITY CALLS (GRADES K–2)

RT 4

Purpose: To increase students' awareness of the behavior of responsibility.

Materials:

RT2d

RT2e

- Stopper and Starter (RT2d and RT2e) signs; the word "Responsible" printed on the red stopper sign; the words "Not Responsible" printed on the green starter sign. Tape signs on rulers or paper towel tubes.

- Two (or more) toy telephones.

- A set of problems whose solutions involve either responsible or irresponsible actions. Each problem is printed on an index card (problems you might use for this activity are given below).

- Six to ten index cards; using crayons, draw a green one-inch dot in the middle of half the cards and a red one-inch dot on the other half.

Procedure: The teacher can choose to give the directions or use the Able Puppet for this purpose. Explain that when we act in the right way and are accountable or dependable, we are acting "responsibly." Hold up the green starter sign with the word "Responsible." Tell students the word responsible is on the green sign to remind us to "go" and keep acting responsibly. Ask children to describe a few behaviors that are responsible.

Tell students that when we behave in ways we know are not right, this behavior is called "Not Responsible." Hold up the red stopper sign with the word "Not Responsible." Explain that the word is printed on a red sign to remind us to "stop and think" before we act irresponsibly. We can choose how we act. Briefly discuss kinds of behaviors that are not responsible.

Hang up the "Responsible" and "Not Responsible" signs. Show students the index cards with the green and red dots and then shuffle them face down. Place the problem cards in a separate pile face down. Explain that students will be playing a game. If they pick a card with a green dot they are to act responsibly. If they choose a card with a red dot they are to act irresponsibly. Tell students they are to take turns picking a card; they are to keep the color a secret and then choose a problem card. Ask individual students to draw a problem card and read it aloud. Students then use the telephone to show what they would do, whom they would call, and what they would say. Here are some suggested problem situations:

- You're at home alone with a friend. You think you smell smoke.

- You are with your friend at the park and he (or she) falls out of the swing. Your friend is not moving and looks very hurt.

- Your neighbor's kitten is stuck in a tree. They're not at home.

- Your dog gets out of your yard. You can't find him.

- You forget about the bath you started, until you see water seeping out from under the bathroom door.

- Your friend leaves her homework at your house.

- Your friend just came over and wants you to quickly go to his house. Your parents said you are to watch the cake cooking in the oven. Your friend says you'll only be gone a minute.

- You see your dog dig up your neighbor's new flowers in the front yard and put them in your backyard.

- You forgot what page you're supposed to do for math.

For younger students:

- Able is unhappy; he doesn't want to shine today.

- Able sees two stars are about to collide.

- Able gets lost and can't find his way back to his galaxy.

- Able forgets to thank a friend for a present and his friend gets angry.

- A friend offers to give Able the answers to their astronomy test coming up next week so he won't have to study.

RESPONSIBILITY: A THOUGHT FOR THE DAY   RT 5

Purpose: To enhance students' awareness of responsibility through literacy.

Materials:
- A Thought For the Day (RT5a); one per student (optional).

- Responsibility Thoughts (RT5b); one per student (optional).

- *For younger students:* Able Puppet (RT1b).

RT5b

RT5a

Procedure: There are dozens of possibilities for using the following quotations on responsibility. You may wish to write one "Thought A Day" on the board for students to discuss at a Class Meeting or in the Journal. Some teachers have students keep a notebook of thoughts. Each day students copy the quotation on their worksheets and then write or draw a personal reflection about what the quotation means to them.

Bulletin Board: Expand the "Thought for the Day" activity to a bulletin board. Cut out and post on the board the words: "Responsibility Thoughts." Then, begin to print a few quotations on responsibility on colored paper and pin them to the board. Encourage students to be on the lookout for responsible thoughts and deeds and then add them to the board. You may want to add pictures of a few of the famous authors to accompany their words. Finally, ask students to write their own definitions of responsibility on colored paper and to add these to the famous authors.

Able STAR Shape Book: To adapt the activity for younger children, consider making Able STAR Shape Books. Duplicate a copy of the Able Puppet on light-colored cardstock-weight or construction paper. Insert several pages of plain paper or writing paper between the Able Puppet cover and staple along the top or sides. Students can draw, write, or dictate their thoughts about responsibility each day responsibility is discussed in class.

RESPONSIBILITY VOCABULARY RT 6

Purpose: To expand students' vocabulary using terminology on the theme of responsibility.

Responsibility Vocabulary:

Week 1: Responsible

Week 2: Trustworthy

Week 3: Rules

Week 4: Covenant

Thought: *Language is the dress of thought.*—Samuel Johnson

RT6

Materials:

- Bookmark corresponding to the vocabulary word of the week (RT6); one per student copied on light-colored cardstock-weight paper.

- Chart paper and pens, or blackboard and chalk.

Procedure: Explain that each week you will feature a different key vocabulary term that relates to the theme of responsibility. Give a copy of the Responsibility Bookmark to each student. Tell students to study the words on the list. Whenever they learn a new word, they should add it to their bookmark.

Vocabulary Extensions: Each week a different key vocabulary word could be written on a large piece of chart paper. As students develop new words, these could be added to the list. Some teachers use the lists as spelling lists or vocabulary drills. Words could also be used in creative writing or in ways that develop students' knowledge of antonyms and synonyms.

School-Wide Adaptations: Many schools feature a Word of the Week that focuses on the monthly theme. Print one word for each week on paper banners and hang them on school walls.

RESPONSIBILITY CONTRACT

RT 7

Purpose: To increase students' awareness of the importance of responsibility.

Thought: *Ability will enable a man to get to the top, but it takes character to keep him there.*—Proverb

Materials for the Center:

- Bulletin board, cardboard carrel or table top.

- 16 task cards, cut and laminated.

- Shoe box or card stand to store task cards.

- Responsibility Contract (RT7); one per student.

- Miscellaneous supplies including glue, scissors, hole punch, stapler, yarn, construction paper scraps, pencils, tape, crayons and marking pens.

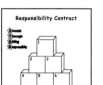

RT7

Materials for the Tasks:

- Task 1: shoebox, paper scissors, marking pens, and glue.

- Task 2: plain paper, pens or pencils.

- Task 3: wire hanger; tagboard templates (at least 6" in the following shapes—circle, triangle, square, and diamond), magazines, paper, paper punch, and string.

- Task 4: paper, pens or pencils, computer (optional).

- Task 5: 3" x 6" strip of butcher paper or adding machine paper, pencil, tape, and colored pencils or crayons.

- Task 6: paper tubes from a wire hanger; material (cardboard, burlap, cloth, wallpaper, or construction paper), paints, crayons, tape, and string.

- Task 7: construction paper, crayons, felt pens, magazines, and cut-outs.

- Task 8: paper, pens, pencils, computer (optional), and want-ads from the newspaper.

- Task 9: construction paper, glue, magazines, and scissors.

- Task 10: construction paper, pencils, felt pens, scissors, paper punch, and yarn.

- Task 11: construction paper, felt pens, crayons paint, magazine cut-outs, and templates.

- Task 12: magazine cut-outs, newspaper words, glue, paste, scissors, felt pens or crayons.

- Task 13: construction paper, glue, magazines, felt pens, crayons, a dictionary, and scissors.

- Task 14: scissors, 12" x 18" construction paper, pen, pencil or marking pens.

- Task 15: marking pens, ruler, 6" x 18" construction paper, and scissors.

- Task 16: paper and pencils.

Procedure: If you have limited space or do not have a permanent classroom, consider stocking a box with art supplies that can be taken out or brought with you each time you do a Character Builder activity.

Set up the Center display in a convenient area of your classroom. Duplicate a copy of the Responsibility Contract for each student and store it in the center.

Mount the task cards (1-16) on heavy paper. Cut them in half and laminate for durability. Store all the materials needed to complete the tasks at the Center (these are indicated on the tasks cards as well as in the list above).

Students may complete the tasks in any order. Upon completion of the task, students color in the corresponding task card number on the Responsibility Contract.

Dioramas 1

1. Cut a small peephole in the end of a box with a removable lid.

2. Make a slot in the top of the box to let in light.

3. Cut along three sides of the slot and fold back the flap.

4. Inside the box, make a scene that shows you acting responsibly. Show in the scene how the trait of responsibility can have a positive impact.

You need: paper, scissors, marking pens, glue and a box with a removable lid.

Letter to a Friend 2

Dear Friend,

1. Write a letter to a friend, telling the person about responsibility. What are the three most important things about responsibility you want your friend to know?

2. If necessary, use the sample letter below to help.

_____ (Date)
_____ (Your address)
_____ (Your city and state)

Dear _____ ,
_____
_____
_____

_____ Sincerely, (or Love,)
_____ (Your name)

Responsibility Mobile 3

1. Cut out at least four shapes from heavy paper and use the templates to trace around them.

2. On the front of each shape, draw or cut out pictures or words that describe responsibility.

3. On the back of the shape, tell how the picture represents responsibility.

4. Tie your shapes to the hanger.

   You need: paper, paper punch, magazines, templates.

Responsibility Commercial 4

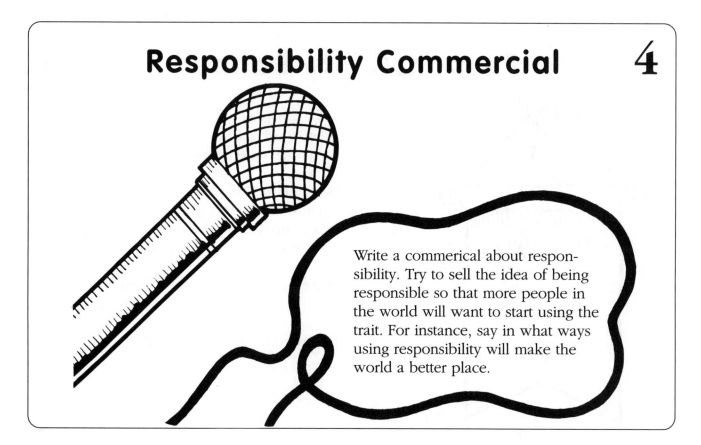

Write a commerical about responsibility. Try to sell the idea of being responsible so that more people in the world will want to start using the trait. For instance, say in what ways using responsibility will make the world a better place.

Responsibility Story 5

1. To make a movie about responsibility, cut a long strip of butcher paper 3" × 36" (or use adding machine tape).

2. Roll each of the ends around a pencil and tape the ends to the pencil.

3. Use crayons, colored pencils or ink pens to draw a scene of what responsibility looks and sounds like in action.

4. Roll up the movie to tell the story to a friend.

Responsibility Banner 6

1. Make a banner about responsibility from a material such as cardboard, burlap, cloth, wallpaper, or construction paper.

2. Decorate the banner with pictures, words or cut-outs about responsibility using paint, paper cut-outs, stitchery, yarn, felt-tipped pens, magazines, or crayons.

3. Staple or tape your finished banner to a paper tube from a wire clotheshanger.

4. Tie on both ends and hang it up.

Responsibility Books 7

1. Visit a library or bookstore and ask for recommendations of good books that deal with responsibility.

2. Choose one of these books to read.

3. Now make a book cover. Be sure to include the title and author and an illustration showing what responsibility looks like. On the back of the book cover describe how responsibility is shown in the story using construction paper, crayons, felt pens, magazines, and cut-outs.

Responsibility Want Ad 8

WANTED:

A Responsible Person

Someone who is trustworthy and dependable. This person can be counted on to follow through on whatever tasks they're asked to do. They turn in their assignments on time. They always do what is right.

1. Pretend you are advertising in the newspaper for someone who demonstrates responsibility. You'll want people to know why the trait is important, what it looks and sounds like. How will you describe responsibility to people?

2. In 30 words or less, write an ad for the newspaper.

Responsibility Poster   9

1. Cut out pictures from magazines of things that show responsibility.

2. Paste the pictures onto a large sheet of construction paper.

3. Write the word "Responsibility" at the top of the paper.

4. Print the definition of responsibility somewhere on the poster.

You need: magazines, scissors, glue, construction paper.

Responsibility Hanging   10

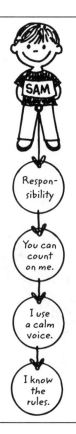

1. Make a paper figure of yourself and color it.

2. Cut four 6" circles out of paper.

3. On the first circle write the word "Responsibility."

4. On each of the three remaining circles, write or draw a different way you can speak or act in a responsible manner. What does the trait look like and sound like?

5. Punch a hole in the middle of the top and bottom of each circle. Punch one hole in your figure.

6. Tie 5" yarn pieces in the holes to connect the holes.

Campaign Poster 11

1. Make a campaign poster about responsibility.

2. Make sure you include the word "Responsibility" and two reasons why someone would want to vote for having responsibility at your school.

You could use: construction paper, felt pens, crayons, paint, magazine cut-outs and templates.

(See RT7a for a full-page example.)

Responsibility Portraits 12

1. Draw a picture of your head and cut it out. Or make your silhouette by standing in front of an overhead projector. Have a friend trace the silhouette that appears on a piece of paper taped on the wall.

2. Cut out your silhouette. Think about yourself when you are acting and speaking responsibly. Use words and/or pictures to describe these moments.

You could use: magazine cut-outs, newspaper words, glue, paste, scissors, felt pens or crayons.

Responsibility Pennant 13

1. Make a pennant about responsibility.

2. Inside the pennant write the definition of responsibility.

3. Now write a least three words that mean almost the same thing as responsibility.

4. Illustrate responsibility with a picture or magazine cut-out. What does responsibility look like?

You could use: construction paper, glue, magazines, felt pens, crayons, a dictionary, scissors.

Responsible Sayings 14

1. Cut out a large speech bubble from construction paper.

2. Think about what responsibility sounds like. Write at least five things someone would say who sounds responsible.

You need: scissors, 12" × 18" construction paper, pen, pencil or marking pens.

Responsibility Bumper Sticker 15

1. Design a bumper sticker about responsibility.

2. Include on the bumper sticker:

    a. the word "Responsibility"

    b. a motto or slogan for why you should use it

    c. at least three words that describe it

You need: marking pens, ruler, 6" × 18" construction paper, scissors.

Responsibility Rap 16

1. Make up a rap about responsibility.

2. The rap must have at least 10 lines describing why responsibility is important.

3. Write the finished rap on paper.

4. Be ready to present the rap to the group.

 **3**

Rules and Responsibilities

CHARACTER BUILDER STEP #2:

- Enhance Awareness of Rules and Responsibilities

KEY OBJECTIVES:

- Setting Up Class Meetings
- Making Rules
- Shaking on a Pledge
- Using Twelve Inch Voices

3

Rules and Responsibilities

We need to restore the full meaning of that old word, duty.
It is the other side of rights.

—PEARL BUCK

Stanley Coopersmith, a child psychologist at the University of California at Davis, devoted his life's work to the study of self-image. His book, *The Antecedents of Self-Esteem,* has become a landmark in this area. One of Coopersmith's research goals was to try and ascertain what environmental conditions promote high self-esteem. His research team, which studied over 1,700 boys and their families, found that those children with higher self-esteem all had a strong commonality: their environments were those with clear, defined and enforced limits and standards. Their parents were significantly less permissive than parents of children with lower self-esteem. Within the household were fair but reasonable standards and expectations that were consistently reinforced. As a result, the children felt secure.

CHARACTER BUILDER STEP #2

Enhance Awareness of Rules and Responsibilities

The second step to building a climate of responsibility is to help students know exactly what is expected of them. Setting boundaries and providing a thorough explanation of what behaviors and responsibilities you expect of your students provides a degree of emotional safety so that children can grow in the feeling of security and take new risks to expand their repertoire of self. Your "safety net" of clear expectations allows children to learn self-control and in the end accountability: "I am responsible for my behavior."

Coopersmith's research offers the following guidelines for establishing limits and setting guidelines for responsibility in classrooms.

- Base your limits on reasonable and realistic grounds.

- Less is better! Researchers find too often caregivers bombard youth with too many limits and standards. Generally aim for between five and ten, but certainly no more than ten.

- Regulate boundaries with consistency, respect and firmness.

- Set a small number of limits at a time. They can then be maintained more easily without making enforcement into a burdensome way of life.

- Establish clear behavioral consequences when limits are exceeded. These consequences are always best when set ahead of time. Students then know exactly what is expected with no "surprises."

- Some students inevitably will test limits. Remain consistent with your limits. Follow through always with the consequences. Never threaten with loss of acceptance.

- Yes, rules are negotiable. So is life. Once chosen, rules can be modified at any time when you see they're not effective. Ask the student to "state his case." And then listen. Often the student sees a rule's "unfairness" which we may have overlooked. Rules can always be changed or modified.

- Enforce limits nonphysically. Physical consequences will only model to the student physical aggression as the way to solve a problem.

- There are no right rules. Set your expectations for responsibility based on your students' needs and on what will help them succeed.

> "Responsibility for learning belongs to the student, regardless of age."
>
> —Robert Martin

Activities to Enhance Student Responsibility

The activities listed below are taken from the *Esteem Builders* series written by Dr. Michele Borba.

Code	Activity	Page
Activities from Esteem Builders *help students develop an awareness of school rules and appropriate behavior.*		
S15	Rules	57
S16	Scholar Dollars	57
CC1	Beginning Circle Rules	326
SW5	GOTCHA TICKETS	388
Activities from Home Esteem Builders *enhance a school/home partnership regarding student's awareness of school responsibilities.*		
HEB3	What Others Expect of Me	198
HEB4	Rules...Rules...Rules...	199
HEB25	Home Responsibilities	220
HEB26	My Responsibilities from School	221

Home Esteem Builder *Grams to send to parents regarding rules.*

Staff Resources in Staff Esteem Builders.

Staff Development Training Session: Esteem Builders Trainer's Manual.

*For more information about these books, call Jalmar Press at 800/662-9662. They can be purchased individually or in a kit.

CLASS MEETINGS

Many activities in *Character Builders* are based on the learning structure called the Class Meeting. This is a time when all of your students meet to participate in a learning discussion. The benefits of this structure in building the character trait of responsibility are enormous: the meetings encourage student participation, build a feeling of community or inclusion, enhance a positive social climate and establish clear expectations for emotional safety. This first activity creates the "boundaries" and "rules" for Class Meetings as well as establishing basic responsibilities in the classroom. You may wish to add to or delete from this list, but once explained to the students, post it and use it for the duration of the school year.

TWELVE INCH VOICES   RT 8

Purpose: To help students learn the rules and responsibilities for Class Meetings as well as acceptable classroom behavior; to practice "speaking in turn" using 12 inch voices.

Thought: *All learning occurs in a social context.*—Hanoch McCarty

Materials:

- Meeting Rules (RT8); one copy per student and one copy enlarged poster size.

- Responsibility (RT1a); one copy enlarged poster size.

- A 12 inch ruler.

- Strips of poster board cut into 12 inch pieces; one per student.

- Stop watch (optional).

- Chalk and chalkboard, or chart paper and marking pens.

RT8

RT1a

Class Meeting Rules

Raised hand = quiet.

Use calm, 12 inch voices.

Listen attentively.

Extinguish putdowns.

Speak in turn.

Procedure: Begin by establishing the seating arrangement for all Class Meetings. This might be with all students seated in a circle on the floor, with student chairs in a circle, or with student desks in a circle or U-shape. Prearrange this format. Ideally circles are set in "class meeting style" so students can see each other's faces.

Ask students to sit in a Class Meeting circle. Explain: "This year our class will be working together in ways that may be different from other teachers. We will meet often as a whole class talking together in a Class Meeting Circle like this." Explain that sometimes a Class Meeting will be held to discuss school issues. Other times students will meet to learn new skills that will help them learn better not only in school but in life. Emphasize the Class Meeting is a time when students can share ideas and concerns. It is also a time to take responsibility for making sure everyone feels as though their rights are being met.

Post the Meeting Rules on the board and explain that these are the responsibilities or behaviors that are expected of students whenever they meet together. Emphasize that Meeting Rules apply not only to the whole class but to a group as small as two students. Briefly describe each rule as follows. *(Note: To adapt the activity for younger students, consider having the Able Puppet act out each rule.)*

- ***Raised hand = quiet.*** Tell students whenever you raise your hand in the circle or in the classroom it is a non-verbal signal that means everyone stop talking and please raise their hand, too. Explain you will never have to say anything to tell students to stop talking. They are expected to immediately stop any conversation or work, raise their hand and look up. Everyone will then wait with their hands up until all the class is doing the same. Practice the technique a few times with students. Younger students enjoy being timed with a stop watch to see their "freeze and be quiet" time improve with each practice.

- *Use calm, 12 inch voices.* Ask students what they think a calm, 12" voice looks like and sounds like. Emphasize that 12" voices should not be heard by anyone further away than 12 inches. Distribute 12" paper strips to each student. Hold up a 12" ruler and show students that their paper strip is the same length as your 12" ruler. Ask students to find a partner sitting next to them. For one minute ask students to take turns holding the 12" paper strip slightly lower than the mouths of the partners to practice speaking in 12" voices. Have students take turns with their partner using 12" voices and telling one another the first two rules of the Meeting Rules.

- *Listen attentively.* Explain that students have the right to be heard in this classroom but they also have the responsibility to listen politely to the opinion of others. This rule means that whenever anyone is speaking--a student, a teacher, a parent, the principal--it is everyone's responsibility to give the speaker their full attention with their eyes as well as ears. Emphasize that to really understand someone's message we need to pay attention not only to their words but also to their feelings.

- *Extinguish put-downs.* Tell students you want the classroom and school to be a safe place where everyone can feel good about being here. Explain that every individual has the right to be treated with dignity and respect. It is everyone's responsibility to treat everyone else with the same respect. Put-downs (statements that hurt people's feelings) are not allowed.

- *Speak in turn.* Finally, everyone's ideas and opinions are given equal importance in the classroom. The expectation is that when someone is speaking he or she is not to be interrupted. This shows respect to the person speaking.

Ask students if they would like to include any other rules that might help them feel emotionally safe during future Class Meetings. Any new rules agreed upon by the class could be added to the Meeting Rules.

Distribute a copy of the Meeting Rules to students still sitting in the circle. Ask students to find a partner sitting on either their left or right. Make sure all students have partners, then ask them to practice saying the rules.

Completed forms are put into their Character Builder Notebooks.

School-Wide Ideas: Many schools have incorporated the class Rules and Responsibilities school-wide so that all students use the same rules.

- *12 Inch Voice Rule.* To remind students to use quieter indoor voices, the staff at Hawthorne School in Mesa, Arizona, printed up dozens of 8" × 4" construction paper signs and then folded them in half. The message said: "Use quiet 12 inch voices, please." They placed them on each library and cafeteria table school-wide. The common language they used to remind students to use quiet voices was "use 12 inch voices." Was it effective? Yes! Not only did everyone at the school know what a 12 inch voice was, but everyone used it!

- *High Four Rules.* Crest View School in Brooklyn Park, Minnesota, created High Four Rules for their students. They taught the rules to all students and staff at a student assembly. The benefit was instantaneous. Everyone shared the same common language and signal as a reminder. Students say the High Four Rules while holding their palm up, thumb folded inside so four fingers remain. Each of the four fingers stands for one of the four High Four Rules. Three variations of the High Four Rules are below. Remember, there's no "right or wrong" set of rules. The key points of effective rules are to choose ones important to your students, make sure they are fair and understood, and implement them consistently.

F	**f**ollow directions and respect others.
O	**o**bjects, hands and feet to myself.
U	**u**se positive language.
R	**r**emember supplies and material.

F	**f**ace the speaker.
O	**o**nly the speaker should be talking.
U	**u**se your best listening position.
R	**r**aise your hand.

F	**f**eet, hands and objects in your own space.
O	**o**rganize supplies to be ready for class.
U	**u**se appropriate language.
R	**r**espect others.

CLASS MEETING RULES   RT 9

Purpose: To create a secure learning environment where students know what is expected; to hold the first Class Meeting in which the Meeting Rules are practiced; to introduce the concept of the Talking Stick to help students speak in turn (optional).

Materials:

- Meeting Rules (RT8); one copy enlarged poster size (optional).

- Class Meeting Notes (RT9); one copy per student.

- A stick (i.e. dowel, ruler or branch) 12 inches long.

- *For younger students:* Able Puppet head (RT1b) on a 12 inch dowel or ruler.

RT9

RT8

RT1b

Procedure: Briefly review the Class Meeting Rules from the previous session as a group. Ask each student to use a 12 inch voice, turn to a nearby partner and take turns stating the rules.

Explain that your expectation is to have a great year together where students not only will be successful learners but also learn to respect one another. Say, "We need to begin by finding out about each other." Write the first Class Meeting topic on the board: "One thing about

"You can't escape the responsibility of tomorrow by evading it today."

—Abraham Lincoln

me I'd like you to know..." Tell the class each person will introduce themselves first with their name and then tell one thing they would like others to know about them. Examples include an interest, a hobby, places they have lived or traveled to.

Model the topic by sharing something about yourself: "Hello, I'm Mrs. Jones and one thing I'd like you to know about me is that I love to ski." It will then be the next person's turn to speak until everyone in the circle has shared. Tell students, "If you don't wish to take a turn simply say 'pass' and we hope you'll share the next time."

Explain that each person will speak in turn moving clockwise around the group. You may wish to quietly review the list of Meeting Rules. Then tell students that to help everyone remember to "speak in turn" the class will be using a "talking stick." This stick may be a ruler, a dowel, or a branch about 12 inches in length. Explain that "talking sticks" are an old Indian custom in which an object, such as a peace pipe, stick or rope was passed around a campfire. Each person had a chance to add to the story as they held the stick and then passed it to the person to their left. *For younger students, say, "Today, our 'talking stick' will be Able the Shooting Star Puppet to remind us to use 12 inch voices and listen attentively to the person who speaks."*

Conclude the activity by thanking the students for their thoughts. You could ask students to turn to the two people sitting next to them and thank them for their ideas.

RT9

Write on the blackboard or chart paper the sentence stem: "One thing I learned about a friend...." Provide each student a copy of the Meeting Notes (RT9). Ask them to fill in the date and meeting topic and to complete the sentence stem. Completed Meeting Note forms are inserted in students' Character Builder Notebook.

Additional Class Meeting Topics: The possibilities for meeting and discussion topics are endless. Consider using any of the activities in *Character Builders* for a Class Meeting.

SCHOLAR DOLLARS   RT 10

Purpose: To familiarize students with school/class rules; to reinforce positive behavior with concrete rewards.

Thought: *If some people got their rights they would complain of being deprived of their wrongs.*—Oliver Herford

Materials: Scholar Dollars (RT10). Have on hand a plentiful supply of Scholar Dollars. Make copies of the form on ditto paper. Use a paper cutter to cut individual dollars along the lines. Store the cut dollars in an accessible box or basket.

Rules Poster: Each classroom rule will require one piece of 12" × 18" light-colored poster-board. Using thick-colored marking pens, print the classroom rule on the posterboard. For younger students you may wish to depict the rule in pictorial form. Use either a hand-drawn picture or Polaroid picture of students correctly demonstrating the rule. Assign each rule a number, and print it on the poster so it is clearly visible.

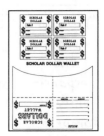

RT10

Scholar Dollar Wallet. Make a wallet from a piece of light-brown construction paper for each student to store their "dollars." Fold and cut it as described in the directions.

Awards: Make available various awards for students to buy with their Scholar Dollars. Each award should be clearly marked with a price tag or sticker as to how much it would cost. Set prices in relation to how often you plan to distribute Scholar Dollars and the cost of the item.

Procedure: Discuss each rule again with the students. Post the rules around the room at a visible location. Explain that you will be watching for students who follow the rules. Whenever you see such behavior, hand the student a Scholar Dollar. The student must now correctly identify which of the rules he/she thinks the rule was that the teacher was reinforcing with him/her, and signs the form.

Students should keep their dollars in the wallets. (It may be better for younger students to give their dollars to you for safekeeping.) At a convenient time, consider having a quick Scholar Dollar evaluation time. Students who earned a dollar now report to the class which rule they think they were demonstrating when they were awarded the dollar. Students keep all awarded dollars until they wish to "spend" them at the class store. Assign special "buying times."

RESPONSIBILITY BENEFITS   RT 11

Purpose: To help students understand the benefit or value of rules.

Thought: *What men value in the world is not rights, but privileges.*—H.L. Mencken

Materials: Chalk and chalkboard, or chart paper and felt pens.

Procedure: Ask students to join you in a circle and review the rules and responsibilities for the Class Meeting. Write the term "rule" on a chart or the board and ask for meanings from students. Responses: "rule \ n: prescribed guide for conduct or action." Now ask students to think of instances where there are rules. These examples could be written on chart paper. Responses include driving rules, voting age, drinking age, marriage license, skate boarding, bicycle riding, bicycle helmets, traffic signs, playground rules, and fire safety rules.

Tell students that they are capable of taking responsibility for creating some of their own rules. They will have that opportunity sometime this week. Before writing rules, it's often helpful to talk about the benefit of rules. Dozens of possible classroom meeting topic regarding rules are provided. Choose one or two for each Classroom Meeting. Students can also use these as journal topics stored in their Character Builder Notebook.

Suggested Topics on Rules

- Can you use the same rules at home and at school? If so, which ones. If not, why not?

- Should teachers/parents make different rules for different ages?

- Who should make rules?

- What are the most important rules for safety?

- What rules would help students learn more?

- Name one (school or home) rule that you agree with. Why?

- If you could set rules, what new rules would you make for members of your family...the school...the community....the country?

- What rules should both teachers and children have to follow in school?

- What rules (if any) should both adults and children/parents and children follow?

- How might the world be different if both adults and children followed the same rules?

- Is there a need for authority?

- Would you rather have no rules at all or live with the rules you have now?

- What would happen if there were no rules?

- If there weren't any rules, what would you do differently?

- Could people live in a society with no rules?

- Is there a best way to decide on rules? What is it?

- What makes a good rule?

- What should happen if someone broke a rule?

- Is there an alternative to prison?

- If you were a parent, what rules would you set?

- If you were President, what would be your first rule?

- If there could be only one rule in a school, what would the best rule be?

- The definition of a rule is to exercise authority or power over; to control, direct or guide. Is authority the best way to rule?

- Name at least three countries that govern strictly by authority. What is their form of government called?

- What is the difference between autocracy and democracy?

Follow-Up Discussions. The discussion of rules and responsibilities can easily be integrated into history. The following list of famous rule makers, rules and rule-making groups is provided as additional resources.

Famous Rule Makers

Abraham Lincoln
Jimmy Carter
Benjamin Franklin
James Madison
Alexander Hamilton
Thomas Jefferson

Famous Rules

Golden Rule
Magna Carta
Rights of Children
Emancipation Proclamation
Declaration of Independence
Constitution

RESPONSE
+
ABILITY

Rule-Making Groups

Congress
Supreme Court
Judicial System
City Council
Board of Directors
School Board
United Nations

Rule Concepts

authority
justice
privacy
responsibility
freedom
diversity
property
republic
federation
autocracy
government
commonwealth
monarchy

RESPONSIBILITY

Follow-up Activity. Students can interview different adults (student, staff member or parent) regarding the rule topic of the day. Each interview can be written up and included in the students' Character Builder Notebooks or the main idea briefly summarized at a Class Meeting.

MAKING RULES   RT 12

Purpose: To set the stage for students generating their own agreed upon rules for responsible behavior at school or in class; to help students recognize the benefit of rules.

Thought: *I leave this rule for others when I'm dead: Be always sure you're right–then go ahead.*—Davy Crockett

RT12

RT1d

Materials:

- Making Rules (RT12)

- Looks Like/Sounds Like (RT1d)

- Blackboard and chalk, or chart paper and felt pen.

Procedure: Gather students for a Class Meeting and briefly review the rules and responsibilities from Making Rules (RT12). Explain to students that you feel they are capable of taking responsibility for some of their own classroom rules. Today's Class Meeting will help "set the stage" for a next session when they will form their own rules. The following kinds of questions may help guide students into recognizing the benefits of rules and set the stage for students to create their own class rules. If working with older students, appoint two of the students to serve as "recorders" and to summarize speakers' main ideas.

- What are rules?

- Why do we have rules?

- What are examples of rules for the home? school? community?

- What happens when rules are broken? Why?

- What would life be like without rules?

Note: Help students recognize that without rules, people could get hurt and not feel "safe." Knowing that you have the choice to be responsible to yourself and others helps you succeed.

RT12

Ask students to pretend they are members of Congress and are responsible for making rules for the country. What might the process of rule making "look like and sound like?" Create a T-chart for rule making based on student ideas such as the one that follows. Students can later make a copy of the Making Rules (RT12) or the Looks Like/Sounds Like Chart (RT1d) and file them in their Character Builder Notebook.

Rule Making

 Looks Like   **Sounds Like**

Looks Like	Sounds Like
Writing down ideas	"What do we need to be safe?"
Nodding	"What will help us learn?"
Smiling	"What do we agree on?"
Puzzled faces	"What do you think?"
Shaking hands	"This is what I wish..."
Tallying votes	"These are our rules."
Eye contact	"One thing I need..."
Leaning in	"I'd like to add..."

Student-Designed Rules and Responsibilities

Many researchers feel that it is critical for students to take an active role in the formation of any guidelines that might affect them. Constructed in this way, rules are then seen by the students as "owned." The following activity helps students formulate classroom or school rules that will guide their behavior. Robert Ellington, a consultant, suggests incorporating five general concepts as a format for the rules:

1. Truth
2. Trust
3. Responsibility
4. Active Listening
5. No Put-downs

Add any other categories you consider important to your environment. Encourage students to come up with their own wording for rules using each of the concepts.

You might wish to keep the following suggestions for "effective rules" in mind as you guide students through the rule-setting process. Students may then vote on the wording they feel best suits each category.

"The responsibility of the great states is to serve and not to dominate the world."

—Harry S. Truman

Effective Rules

rule \ n: prescribed guide for conduct or action

The best rules are . . .

- formed on beliefs
- written positively whenever possible
- clear and concise, in "black-and-white" terms
- written in student terminology, understandable
- specific so the child can easily see a correlation when behavior violates a rule
- written in behavioral terms
- enforceable
- limited to only the ones most needed.

SETTING OUR RULES AND RESPONSIBILITIES

RT 13

Purpose: To provide the opportunity for students to create their own class/school responsibilities.

Thought: *If we are ever in doubt about what to do, it is a good rule to ask ourselves what we shall wish on the morrow that we had done.*—John Lubbock

RT13a

Materials:

- Brainstorming Rules (RT13a)

- Responsibility Covenant (RT13b)

- Chart paper and marking pens, or blackboard and chalk.

Procedure: Invite students to join you for a Classroom Meeting. Tell them that a classroom/ school is like a community. It, too, needs rules to help students get along and have a happy and safe place.

RT13b

Explain to students that they will now be brainstorming all the possible rules that might help the classroom/school be a happier place where students can learn. Use the Brainstorming Rules poster to remind students no put-downs are allowed in brainstorming. All ideas count and are written down. The four questions below can be used to guide students in brainstorming rules. Keep asking students: "What rules do you need to help you feel safe/get along/learn best?" Write all ideas on the board. Older students can write down the ideas on the chalkboard. Guide students in some areas which may be overlooked. Set a time limit of no more than five minutes. One child can serve as the "time keeper."

- What classroom/school rule would help you/everyone learn more?

- What classroom/school rule would help everyone get along better?

- What do you need to help you feel safe at this school?

- What rule would help our classroom/school be a happier/better place?

Now ask students to discuss the pros and cons of each option. Eliminate any ideas that are repetitive. Aim for a student-generated list of no more than five to eight items. Explain to students the list may be added to or changed at any time.

RESPONSE + ABILITY

Tell students that in a democracy the "majority wins." Ask students to take a final time to state their pro or con opinion on any items on the chart. Finally, students vote on the list until it is chosen by a clear majority.

Compile a final list called "Our Responsibilities" or another term chosen by the students and copy onto chart paper. Write the list on the form Responsibility Covenant (RT13b) and make a copy for students to take home and share with their parents.

Teacher Ideas:

- *Personally Important Rule.* Some teachers begin classroom rule formation by listing the one or two rules personally important to the students. These two rules are "automatic." Class rules are then the "joint" rules of the teacher and students.

- *Class Constitution.* One teacher begins the student rule-making process by relating the idea of a Class Constitution. She divides students into small groups to develop a list of rules based on student needs. The sentence stem "In order for people to learn and be safe…" helps generate ideas from students which are then listed on the board. The five rules that receive the most votes from students are added to the list of classroom rules. *Idea suggested by fourth grade teacher, T. Gayla Miller of New York.*

- *One Rule I Need.* If a teacher finds there's a rule the class didn't add but he or she feels is important, it's added to the listed by stating, "There's one rule I need because…"

- *School-Wide Rules.* Jefferson Elementary in Hays, Kansas, kicked off their site's first theme, "Positive Attitude," by asking the students to help them write rules all staff and students would follow—rules that would display the school's identity to all who entered the building. Each class developed its own list of rules. The entire school then came together for an assembly to discuss their choices.

"The staff discussed with the students how similar the lists were from class to class," said Jefferson school psychologist Karen Wasinger. "The staff then condensed the lists into one that everyone would follow. The students had great input. They essentially chose the rules they were to live by."

The rules were sent home with the students so parents could see what was expected of their children during the school day. "By asking the students to write their own rules, we have given them ownership in their learning process. They are proud to be students at Jefferson and they really reflect a positive attitude," Wasinger said. "The staff must also follow the school rules and model a positive attitude at all times. If we can't do it, we can't expect our students to do it either."

At Jefferson, we:

Are respectful to self, others, and property.

Use kind words and actions.

Walk, work, and play safely.

Use appropriate voices.

Are good listeners.

Follow directions.

Use time wisely!

RESPONSIBILITY COVENANT

RT 14

Purpose: To familiarize students and parents with class/school expectations of their responsibilities.

Thought: *Effective discipline programs provide clear and specific rules along with guidelines for enforcement without sacrificing the higher levels of learning that principles provide.*—Richard Curwin and Allen Mendler, authors of *Discipline with Dignity*

RT13b

RT14

Materials:

- Responsibility Covenant (RT13b); one per student.

- Pledge Shake (RT14); one copy enlarged poster size.

Procedure: Ask students to copy the finalized rules they created from a previous activity onto the Responsibility Covenant form (for younger or nonwriting students you'll need to write the finalized list on the form). You may wish to have each student meet with you briefly to describe the rules back to you. Students can also practice saying the rules to a partner.

When you recognize that the student understands the rules, sign the form together on the line provided, then ask the student to demonstrate to you the gesture of commitment, The Pledge Shake.

The student takes the form home to discuss the rules with a parent or guardian who in turn signs the form. The student returns the signed form, which is kept in the student's Character Builder Notebook.

WHAT'S YOUR OPINION?

RT 15

Purpose: To help students recognize the benefit of rules from someone else's point of view.

Materials: Blackboard and chalk, or chart paper and felt pens.

Procedure: Arrange for adults representing a variety of occupations and lifestyles to share their opinion regarding rules and responsibilities at a Class Meeting. Guests could include other staff members, administrators, parents, police officers, bus drivers, yard duty supervisors, secretaries, community officials, doctors, lawyers, judges, and fire officials.

At a Class Meeting prior to the visit of a guest, guide students in creating a list of interview questions. Write these questions on the blackboard or on the chart paper. Questions might include:

- What do you do?

- What are your job responsibilities?

- Who are you responsible to?

- What type of expectations do people have regarding your work?

- Are rules important in your line of work?

- What kinds of rules govern your work?

- What happens if you don't meet the expectation of the people you work for?

- Who makes the rules for your job?

- Is there one rule that seems to be broken the most? Why?

Students take turns during the Class Meeting interviewing the guest. Another version of this activity is to invite several guests on the same day and divide students into small groups. After the guests have left, ask students to summarize each speaker's main idea on a piece of chart paper under the heading, "In My Opinion." After students have listened to a few speakers, they can flip back and forth between the chart pages to notice how points of view differ and how job roles can affect individuals' expectations.

THE PLEDGE SHAKE   RT 16

Purpose: To help students learn the skill of "Coming to an Agreement" or commitment by shaking hands.

Thought: *Commitment: The ability to bind oneself emotionally and intellectually to an idea or task that needs to be completed.*—Webster's Dictionary

Vocabulary: Students can make a list of synonyms and antonyms for the following words: responsibility, reliability, dependability, accountability, trustworthiness, stability, credibility, untrustworthy, thoughtless, unreliable, undependable, and flighty.

RT14

Materials:

- Pledge Shake (RT14) copied on bright-colored paper, one per student, and one copy enlarged poster size (12" × 8" or larger) for the classroom wall.

- Pledge Vocabulary Bookmark (RT6); one per student.

- Blackboard and chalk, or chart paper and colored marking pens.

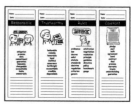

RT6

Procedure: Ask students to form a Class Meeting. Write the term, "Pledge," on the blackboard or chalkboard. Elicit from students the term's meaning. Responses include promise, pact, agreement, and commitment.

Ask a few students to share a time they made a pledge. Explain that a gesture commonly made in our culture to show the other person you agree to the pledge is a handshake. Share The Pledge Shake poster with students. Emphasize that once you make the Pledge Shake it means "There are no take backs" (you can't change your mind). The Pledge Shake means you are committed to your pledge.

Hand each student a personal copy of the Pledge Shake. Ask students to practice the skill with a partner. Explain that students will use the Pledge Shake skill throughout the year (and life) whenever they need to affirm or agree with another person. *Younger students can practice the Pledge Shake with the Able Puppet.*

Take a moment to review the Class Responsibilities. Tell students they have the chance to use the Pledge Shake with the rules they agreed upon as a class. Ask students to say the Class Responsibilities to their partner and then use the Pledge Shake to share their agreement to abide by the class rules.

Ask students to file the skill builder Pledge Shake form in their Character Builder Notebook.

RESPONSIBILITY HANDBOOKS

RT 17

Purpose: To familiarize students with school/class rules and gain an awareness of what they can personally do to act responsibly.

Thought: *People need responsibility. They resist assuming it, but they cannot get along without it.*—John Steinbeck

Materials:
- A strip of poster board (or other heavy paper); one per student. The strips should be about nine inches wide. The length of the strips will depend on the number of school rules (or expectations) decided upon. You will need six inches for each responsibility plus six inches for the cover, for example, sixty-six inches for five rules, forty-two inches for six expectations, and so on.

- A twenty-inch strip of yarn, ribbon, cord or rickrack per booklet.

- Scissors, ruler, stapler, marking pens.

Procedure: Distribute strips and help students mark them into six-inch sections. Then have the students fold their strips accordion style (first section forward, next section back, next forward, and so on). The folds will be crisper and more permanent if creased with a ruler. Staple a twenty-inch piece of yarn to the back cover of each student's booklet for a tie.

Students may now make their Responsibility Handbooks. Explain that each section represents one rule or responsibility. Beginning on the inside of the first section, have students title each section by writing a responsibility or rule. A social skill or character trait for each section are other possibilities for the project. Then have them draw pictorial representations (consider using snapshots or video scanned pictures of the students appropriately demonstrating the behavior) of each responsibility. Finally, students should dictate or write why the expectation is important.

When students complete the interiors of their handbooks have them decorate the covers with self-portraits drawn on skin-colored construction paper. Another possibility is a list of handprinted or computer-generated Class Responsibilities. Cut out the pictures or lists and paste them on decorative backgrounds of each child's choice.

Discuss each rule or responsibility again with the students. Write the responsibilities on chart paper or on the blackboard. Now, explain that responsibilities will never be effective unless students can describe exactly what they can do to behave acceptably.

School-Wide Idea: The staff at Bremerton, Washington, revised the school handbook when they recognized they had too many rules. Instead of dozens of rules, they chose just four responsibilities for the year: Safety, Respect, Responsibility and Effort. Each student wrote or dictated and then illustrated an 8" × 1" page for each of the four guidelines describing what they could personally do to successfully implement the rule. The student-drawn posters were then hung up to decorate the school site. The school appeared warm and structured with dozens of student-made posters of the four themes decorating the walls. Most importantly, students "owned" the responsibilities they depicted.

LIFE RESPONSIBILITY BOOKS RT 18

Purpose: To help students recognize the importance of responsibilities and rules in their own lives.

Thought: *Responsibility: A detachable burden easily shifted to the shoulders of God, Fate, Fortune, Luck, or one's neighbors.*—Ambrose Pierce

Materials:
- Materials for "little books": 6–10 pieces of writing paper and 2 pieces of colored construction paper cut 4" × 6" per student.

- Stapler, colored markers, pens, and crayons.

Literature:
- *Life is Fun* by Nancy Carlson (Puffin, 1993).

Procedure: Share the delightful book, *Life is Fun,* with students. The book begins: "To be happy on earth follow these simple instructions..." What follows are seven rules for making life fun. Ask students to create their own rule book by writing and illustrating each rule on a 4" × 6" piece of paper and stapling the completed pages between a construction paper cover. Each rule should contain either an illustration and/or description of how someone could perform the rule. Rule book title possibilities are endless: class rules, rules for working as a team, personal rules, home rules, rules for the President, parenting rules, or school rules.

RESPONSIBILITY TICKET RT 19

Purpose: To reinforce what responsible behavior looks like in others; to increase responsible behavior school- or class-wide.

Thought: *Taking responsibility means never blaming anyone else for anything you are being, doing, having or feeling.*—Susan Jeffers

Materials:
- Responsibility Ticket (RT19).

RT19

Procedure: Copy the Responsibility Ticket onto light-colored paper and cut along the outside margins. Distribute the tickets in large quantities for staff members and students to use in recognizing positive student expectations. Some teachers like to keep these in supply at a convenient class location for students to send each other.

For younger children, you might use the Able Puppet to explain that one way to be more responsible is to "pay for your own ticket" in life. Every time a student takes a responsible action he/she is buying a ticket. In life a ticket is needed to enter a movie or theme park. The responsibility ticket buys him/her entrance into a higher level of responsibility.

RESPONSIBLE STUDENT PHOTO GALLERY RT 20

Purpose: To recognize students who demonstrate responsible behavior.

Thought: *Men should utter nothing for which they would not willingly be responsible through time and in eternity.*—Abraham Lincoln

Materials:
- A large scrapbook or photo album available at most stationery stores. Write "Responsible Students" on the outside of the album and place it in a convenient location where students can browse.

- A Polaroid camera and film.

- Responsibility Ticket (RT19); photocopy the ticket in large quantities.

- Responsibility Award (RT20); photocopy the award in large quantities.

RT19

Procedure: *(For School-Wide Use)* Develop a bulletin board with a caption such as "Responsible Students" in a highly visible location. Cut construction paper squares slightly larger than a Polaroid snapshot for each day of the school month. Another option is to make a monthly school calendar (at least 46" × 36") on colored butcher paper. Make a caption indicating the month and the targeted school rules, skills or character building themes.

RT20

Distribute a large quantity of the Responsibility Tickets to each staff member. Inform the staff and students (perhaps at a Monthly Theme Assembly) that they may nominate any student for "responsible behavior" as long as they can write the specific behavior that showed responsibility. You might provide an example by completing a ticket with a student: "I saw Robert acting responsibly today because he told the teacher he broke her plant."

When completed, Responsibility Tickets are turned into the office or collected in an envelope designed for filled-in tickets and then carried to the office. Nominated students are called to the office. A group Polaroid snapshot of the "responsible" students is taken and pinned to the calendar on the correct date. The photographs remain until the end of the month when they are removed and pasted in a photo album, perhaps called "The Book of Winners." A calendar for the next school month reinforcing a new school theme is then created and the activity continues for the duration of the school year.

 **4**

Self-Responsibility

CHARACTER BUILDER STEP #3:

- Take Responsibility for Controlling Self

KEY OBJECTIVES:

- Staying Calm and in Conrol
- Apologizing
- Taking Ownership for Inappropriate Behavior
- Recognizing Choices in Behavior

4

Self-Responsibility

*All of us need to know where we end and someone else begins;
we need to understand boundaries. We need to know what is
and is not up to us, what is and is not within our control,
and what is and is not our responsibility.*

—NATHANIEL BRANDON

Learning to stay calm and in control is one of the most effective ways to teach children not only how to behave appropriately but also to take responsibility for their actions. Mature, responsible individuals recognize they must be accountable for their own behavior. They know they have choices on how to respond to any situation, and they can control their anger. Sadly, far too many of today's students are underdeveloped in self-control and are therefore handicapped in developing self-responsibility. One significant contributor to children's inability to stay calm and in control is the constant bombardment of violent images in the media which desensitizes children to aggression. Far too many students today are growing up in fractured childhoods and are unaccustomed to "calm confrontations." The discipline technique too often modeled by parents is yelling, hitting, and swearing. Consider these facts regarding today's students:

- A recent survey revealed a shattering fact: children in the United States are five times more likely to be murdered and 21 times more likely to be shot than children living in the 26 other most industrialized countries in the world.

- A violent crime occurs in our country every 17 seconds, affecting approximately one out of four households.

- In America, a child is reported abused or neglected every 11 seconds.

- In 1995, children 11 years old or younger were responsible for 21 killings; 3,434 assaults; 1,735 robberies; and 435 rapes.

- A child is safer in Northern Ireland than in America.

- Nationwide, the incidence of child abuse has quadrupled since 1975.

- Children in America are at much greater risk than children elsewhere in the advanced industrial world. Compared with other rich countries, children in the United States are much more likely to die before their first birthday; to live in poverty; to be abandoned by their fathers; to be killed before they reach the age of twenty-five.

CHARACTER BUILDER STEP #3

Take Responsibility for Controlling Self

Simply said: a significant number of our students do not know appropriate alternatives for responsible behavior and calming down. It's not a skill that's being modeled in their lives. For these students to ever acquire the trait of responsibility, they must learn how to stay calm and learn the technique of self-control. These are skills that can be taught. It is a skill that will last not only the moments students are in your room but for a lifetime. Years ago, Daniel Webster summed up the critical need to teach our students to take responsibility for their own behavior:

> *Educate your children to self-control ... and you have done much to abolish misery from their future lives and crimes from society.*

We should have heeded those words long ago! It's never too late. This section provides activities to help students learn:

- I am responsible and accountable for my behavior.

- I can stay calm and control my anger.

- I have choices in how I choose to behave.

- I have the responsibility to act in an appropriate manner in the classroom.

- I can apologize for my inappropriate behavior.

The activities in this chapter are designed to help students learn techniques to stay calm and control their anger, recognize they can control their behavior, and learn to be accountable for their behavior.

Activities to Enhance Self-Responsibility

The activities listed below are taken from the *Esteem Builders* series written by Dr. Michele Borba.

For more information on these books, please call Jalmar Press at 800/662-9662.

Esteem Builders

Home Esteem Builders

THE RESPONSIBILITY OF SELF-CONTROL   RT 21

Purpose: To help students learn the responsibility of staying in control.

Thought: *He is the greatest conqueror who has conquered himself.*—Proverb

Materials: "The Responsibility of Self-Control" (RT21); one per student.

Procedure: At a Class Meeting ask students to tell of times when they feel safe and secure. Discuss how students have the right to feel safe, secure and unharmed. Explain that you and the staff will do everything in your power to protect their right to be safe. You might mention and discuss some rules at the school to make sure students are provided these rights.

Emphasize that students also have a responsibility towards others. To make sure everyone feels safe and secure, it is everyone's responsibility to behave in a safe manner and never threaten, hit or hurt anyone else. Tell students that for the next few days you will be discussing ways they can stay calm and control their anger so they can learn to be responsible for controlling themselves. Brainstorm on a chart (or in students' notebooks) ways students can be responsible for the emotional and physical safety of others. Tell students to keep their list of ideas in their Character Builder Notebook.

LOSING CONTROL SIGNALS RT 22

Purpose: To help students learn that they are responsible for controlling their own behavior; to identify body signs that signal loss of control.

Thought: *Anger is just one letter short of danger.*—Anonymous

> **A** — Always stop, think and breathe before taking action.
>
> **N** — No to harming someone or something else.
>
> **G** — Go for help, talk to someone about anger.
>
> **E** — Examine why you're angry.
>
> **R** — Refuse to be part of the violence.
>
> *A poster in the Intervention Room at Crest View
> Elementary School, Brooklyn Park, Minneapolis.*

Materials:

- Stopper (RT2e). One large (36" × 36") "stop sign" duplicated on red construction paper and hung up. A red construction paper "stop sign" (8" × 8"); one per student.

- Thick-tipped black marking pen.

- *For younger students:* Able (RT1b), Spinner (RT22a) and Burner (RT22b) Puppets.

Procedure: Prepare puppets beforehand by duplicating on construction paper and cutting out the patterns. Hang up the large red stop sign shape on a board and in front of the students print inside the shape the word, "Anger." Tell students that all of us have little signs that warn us we're getting angry and out of control. Recognizing these signals helps us think before we act. If we learn to listen to these signs, we can learn to stay in control and act more responsibly. These signs will also help us stay out of trouble.

Spinner, the Out of Control Comet

For younger students, tell the story using Able the Puppet about a time when "a comet named Spinner became angry and lost control. And the comet almost caused Able the Shooting STAR to lose control too. The comet was angry because Able and his star friends had not put out the welcome mat for him. Spinner expected to be given special treatment everywhere he went because he came to visit each galaxy only once every few thousand years. But Able and his friends had been too busy pulling an asteroid out of a black hole, and hadn't even noticed the comet had come by.

"The comet was so angry he rolled himself up into a big red ball and began pulling white hairs out of the top of his fuzzy head. Every once in awhile he spat out a puff of hot air, shooting out a tail of sparks hundreds of feet behind him. Never had he been treated so rudely. How could he let this incident pass? When other galaxies heard about what happened, they would think they could do the same. He decided to make a special trip back to get an apology.

"Having never been out of his orbit, the comet sensed something was terribly wrong when he came close enough to one planet to catch a glimpse of a sign that read, 'End of the world is here.' This was the first time the comet had ever come down a dead-end street. He made a U-turn just in time, which caused a shower of stones to come loose from his tail and fall like hail on the surface of the planet. The comet's face was so flushed and his heart pounding so hard he could hardly see where he was going.

"Able knew trouble was on the horizon when he saw the comet returning with a fiery red face and his tail spitting sparks behind him. Spinner was spinning out of control. In ten minutes, a meteor named Burner was scheduled to come through the galaxy. Able and his friends had rolled out the red carpet for the meteor's arrival, and now the comet was coming in on the same orbit. The two of them were certain to collide.

"When the comet saw the red carpet he assumed it was for himself. 'The stars must have had a change of heart,' he thought. As he flew over the carpet, he felt himself cooling down from his nerve-racking trip through the universe. He was coming in for a smooth landing.

"Able, watching the comet come in, was holding his breath and becoming more and more upset. His heart felt like it would pound right out of his chest. He couldn't think what to do. He imagined himself standing there and watching two out-of-galaxy guests destroy themselves in front of his eyes. The exploding pieces would pierce nearby planets and stars like arrows, and leave scars that would last for centuries. The situation seemed hopeless and out of his control.

"Then Able remembered to breathe deeply to a count of ten . . . '1, 2, 3' . . . he began. When he finished counting to ten, Able felt himself getting back in control. He had an idea. He would pull the red carpet out from under the comet and use it like a matador uses a red flag to send the angry bull charging in his direction. He yanked the carpet aside and the comet came racing after Able with fresh anger over this latest insult. Using the carpet as a shield, Able talked calmly to the comet, telling him he was sorry he missed his earlier visit and that next time the red carpet would be for him. Able kept talking to keep the comet moving in a different direction. Two minutes later the meteor passed right by the spot the comet had been planning to land. When the comet realized what had almost happened, he thanked Able for saving his life."

Tell students they too can learn to stay in control and think how to handle a situation involving a conflict or emergency. The first step is to recognize the signs that tell them when they are angry or upset. Ask (or have the puppet ask) students to think of a time they were angry or mad. Ask, "How did your body feel? How did you know you were angry? These are warning signs." Write students' responses inside the stop sign. Responses include tight muscles, sweating, speaking faster, pounding heart, flushed face or cheeks, ringing in ears, can't think, tight jaws, shouting voice, grinding teeth, clenched hands, tight chest, shaking legs, stomping feet, tense body.

Print a large D in front of the word "anger" so the word now spells "danger." Explain to students these are all danger signs that tell us to stop and think before we lose control.

Provide students with their own red stop sign and ask them to draw or write inside the shape the signal(s) their body gives them that warns "danger" is near because they're starting to get angry. These can be stored in their notebooks or be used for a bulletin board under a caption such as "Danger Signs," or "Anger Is Just One Letter Short of Danger."

For Younger Children: Trace a child's outline on a piece of butcher paper. Paste a smaller stop sign inside the shape and then ask students to show on the paper the different parts of their body that signal the "danger" of approaching anger. Print these responses on the butcher paper next to the body part (i.e. "clenched hands" is written inside the hand shape; "flushed cheeks" is written inside the cheek shape).

STOPPERS AND STARTERS   RT 23

Purpose: To help students distinguish between responsible and irresponsible ways to deal with anger.

Thought: *Be calm in arguing; for fierceness makes error a fault, and truth discourtesy; calmness is a great advantage.*—George Herbert

Materials:
- Masking tape, chalk and eraser, or thick-tipped marking pen and chart paper.

- Character Builder Notebook.

For older students:
- One 8" green and one 8" red construction paper circle. With a thick-tipped black marking pen write the word "Go" inside the green circle and "Stop" inside the red circle.

For younger students:
- Stopper and Starter Signs (RT2d and RT2e); duplicate signs on red and green construction paper and convert into stick puppets by taping them to a ruler, paper towel tube or dowel.

- Able Puppet (RT1b).

Procedure: Gather students in a class meeting. Say, "We all have choices over how we behave when we're upset and tense. Some choices are 'responsible' (as you say the word hang up the green circle on the chalkboard/chart paper near the top). These kinds of

> "Integrity is not a conditional word. It doesn't blow in the wind or change the weather. It is your inner image of yourself, and if you look in there and see a man who won't cheat, then you know he never will."
>
> —John D. MacDonald

behaviors are ones that keep us out of trouble and give others a good impression of us. These behaviors are the right choice and ones we want to keep doing. They're 'starter' behaviors." *For younger students, give examples of the kinds of responsible statements Able would say: "If I calm down, I can think of a way to handle this problem" and "My friends can count on me when they need help."*

Continue explaining, "Sometimes when we're angry we choose the other kinds of behaviors that are 'not responsible.' These behaviors are never the right choices because they can get us in trouble and people think less of us. These are 'stopper' kinds of behaviors." Hang up the red construction paper to the right of the green paper. *For younger students, give examples of the kinds of "not responsible" statements Spinner would say: "I'm so angry I can't see where I'm going," and "I don't care if someone gets hurt when I'm angry."*

Next ask students to brainstorm "not responsible" or "stopper" behaviors that some people choose when dealing with their anger. List these behaviors under the red circle. You might write "not responsible" next to the word. Finally, ask students to list responsible or "starter" behaviors that are acceptable ways to deal with anger. A suggested list is included:

Ways to Deal with Anger

 Responsible   Not Responsible

Tell the person you're angry.	Swear.
Count to 10.	Kick.
Walk away.	Hit something.
Get help.	Throw something.
Draw a picture of your feelings.	Break something.
Hit a pillow.	Hit the person.
Bounce a ball 50 times.	Scream.
Write down how you feel.	Yell.
Talk to a friend.	Say something hurtful.

Ask students to use "A Thought for the Day" (RT5a) page in their notebooks to write about a time when they felt angry.

STAYING CALM AND IN CONTROL   RT 24

Purpose: To help students learn to take responsibility for controlling their behavior by calming down.

Thought: *The greatest cure of anger is delay.*—Seneca

Materials:

- One large (36" × 36") piece of yellow butcher paper cut into a "caution sign" shape (square turned sideways).

- A "caution sign" shape approximately 8" × 8" cut from yellow construction paper; one per student.

- A thick-tipped black marking pen.

- *For younger students:* Able Puppet (RT1b).

Procedure: Gather students in a class meeting and review the anger signals from the preceding lessons. Explain that there are two ways to deal with anger: one is to let it control us (not responsible behavior) and the other is for us to control it (responsible behavior).

Tell students there are dozens of ways to calm down and stay in control (not let anger control us). Ask students to brainstorm responsible ways to control anger and write the responses inside the caution sign. Explain these are ways to "slow down" and use "caution" when students know they feel tense. *For younger students, use the Able Puppet to give a few examples: "I count to 10" and "I take a deep breath."* Other responses include: walk away, turn around, do a jumping jack, talk to someone he/she can trust, think of something else.

Provide each student with a caution sign and ask students to draw or write in the sign the techniques they could use to help them stay in control. The finished signs could be placed in their Character Builder Notebooks or hung up on a bulletin board with a caption such as "Ways to Slow Down."

HANDLING EMOTIONS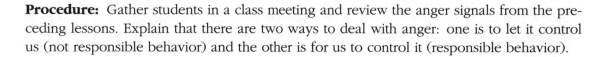

Purpose: To help students explore their feelings and emotions and thereby further develop self-understanding.

Thought: *Never apologize for showing feelings. Remember that when you do, you apologize for the truth.*—Benjamin Disraeli

Materials: A Thought for the Day (RT5a); one per student.

Procedure: Choose any of the following topics for daily journal writing or a class meeting discussion. Students may write their reflections in their journal entry page.

- I feel so mad inside when…

- One time I was really upset was when…

- I seem to get most upset when…

- One way I know I'm angry is when…

- After I'm angry I feel…

- I feel angry when…

- When I'm really angry I…

- I sometimes get mad when…

- What really bothers me is…

YOU'RE IN THE DRIVER'S SEAT

RT 26

Purpose: To help students recognize they have choices over their behavior; to identify techniques that can enable students to stay calm and relaxed.

Thought: *He who does not make a choice makes a choice.*—Anonymous

Materials:
- Marking pen and chart paper, or blackboard and chalk.

For older students:
- Poster board or construction paper, glue, scissors, magazines, marking pens or crayons.

For younger students:
- Ruler, marking pen, 3" circle cut from red construction paper, glue or paste, crayons and a white paper plate. Rule off six "pie sections" on the plate using a ruler and marking pen.

- Able Puppet (RT1b).

Procedure: Gather students in a class meeting and say, "Getting angry is something that happens to everyone. How you deal with your anger will be either responsible or irresponsible. Just remember you always have choices over how you deal with your anger. Responsible people know they're in control."

Give all students the red circle and ask them to draw (or write) something in the middle of the circle that really makes them angry. If students can't think of a specific time, they might draw a picture of themselves when they feel very angry. Next, provide younger students a "sectioned-off" paper plate; provide older students the poster paper. Ask younger students to glue the red circle in the middle of the plate; older students can paste it on the top of their poster. Finally, tell all students, "Remember, you have control over your behavior. It's always hard to stay in control once you're very angry, but if you can take care of yourself and find ways to stay relaxed and calm, you won't be as likely to 'blow up' and get out of control. You're in the driver's seat!"

Brainstorm with all students ways to stay relaxed and calm. *For younger students, use the Able Puppet to give a few examples of how he stays calm: "I talk to my friend, Sparky, who builds me up with positive words," and "I picture everyone in my galaxy getting along."* Ask students, "What things do you do that help you stay calm?" and write their ideas on a chart or blackboard. Ideas might include:

> *"No snowflake in an avalanche ever feels responsible."*
>
> —Stanislaw Jersy Lee

Ways to Stay Calm and Relaxed

- Listen to music.
- Exercise.
- Get to bed earlier.
- Be around people who boost you up.
- Go for a walk.
- Draw pictures of your feelings.
- Talk to someone you trust.
- Eat nutritious food.
- Watch TV shows that aren't violent.
- Picture calm and pleasant scenes in your head.
- Work on your hobby.
- Bounce a ball.
- Read.
- Take a nap.

For younger students: In each section of the paper plate, students choose and draw six ways that help them stay calm and relaxed. Explain that the plate is a steering wheel to remind them they're "in the driver's seat" and have control over their behavior. The red circle picture of their "angry moment" is the warning sign, just like a horn, to remind them to "watch out and beware." Tell students, "If we do things to relax us and keep us calm, we're less likely to get out of control."

For older students: Working alone, in pairs or in teams, students can create a poster (or mural) of "Ways to Stay Relaxed and Calm." The poster might include magazine pictures and words, computer-generated words and student-drawn pictures.

1 + 3 + 10 = CALM

Purpose: To help students learn a technique to stay calm and control their temper.

Thought: *When angry, count to ten before you speak: if very angry, a hundred.*
—Thomas Jefferson

Vocabulary: Control, calm, temper, anger, self-control.

Materials:

- A party size balloon; you will be using the balloon to blow up in front of the students to show how quickly anger can blow up. At this point, pinch the tip of the balloon with your fingers to keep the air in. During the activity you will slowly release air from the balloon to show students how we can stay calm.

- Staying Calm (RT27); one copy per student and one enlarged poster size.

RT27

Procedure: At a Class Meeting discuss the importance of allowing time to cool down and stay calm before students act. Say, "Everybody gets angry and upset at times. The anger inside us can make it hard to stay calm. When we start to lose control and blow up, we can make poor choices and regret how we acted. What's important is to find a way to let the anger out in a responsible way before you pop. Today, we're going to learn a way to stay calm so you can stay in control and out of trouble."

For younger students, adapt the activity slightly by having the Able Puppet role play the activity with the students. The puppet can blow up the balloon and slowly release the air inside as you speak.

Hold up a balloon and slowly blow it up in front of students half way, then stop and pinch the balloon tip to keep the air in. Say, "Anger inside us can blow up very quickly. If we're not careful, it can make us lose our temper and get out of control. Watch what happens." Continue blowing the balloon to full size, stop and again pinch the balloon to hold the air and say, "When there's so much anger in us, it's hard to think and we feel like 'blowing up.' It's hard to stay calm. This is when we make poor choices and get in trouble. We can stay in control by calming down as soon as we start to recognize we're tense and getting upset. Instead of waiting until we feel like 'blowing up,' here's what we can do instead." Refer to Staying Calm form as you say and do the following:

Step 1. "First, tell yourself inside your head to 'calm down.' You might say, 'I am calm and in control.' This lets some of the anger out." Let some of the air out of the balloon. "Keep telling yourself, 'stay calm.'"

Step 2. "Second, slowly take three deep breaths. Take them as deep as you can from the bottom of your stomach. Let each breath out slowly. This will help you calm down and stay in control." As you model taking deep breaths, slowly let more air out of the balloon. It's often helpful to ask students to practice this step with you and place their hands on their stomachs to "feel" the breath.

Step 3. "Finally, count very slowly to 10 inside your head. If you need to, count higher than 10. If that doesn't seem to help, walk away or turn around." Let the remaining air out of the balloon. "Remember, you always have options. Use what will work best for you but stay calm and in control! It means you've learned the responsible trait of self-control."

Now ask students to practice the skill with partners and remind them this skill takes a lot of practice before you can use it when you're very upset. Provide each student with the skill builder, "Staying Calm: 1 + 3 + 10 = Calm."

CALMING DOWN   RT 28

Purpose: To help students learn a strategy for self-control and dealing with their anger.

Thought: *No man can think clearly when his fists are clenched.*—George Jean Nathan

Vocabulary: Self-control, calm, options, anger.

Materials:
- Calming Down (RT28a); one per student and one enlarged poster size.
- Self-Control Plan (RT28b).

Procedure: Introduce the technique for calming down to students. Hang up the chart and write the word "self-control" on the board. Ask students what they think self-control means. Responses include keeping your body in control, having power over your temper, being responsible for your behavior. Teach students the four C-A-L-M steps to self-control.

1. **C = Count** to 10 and say "calm down." Tell students, "When you feel you're getting upset the first thing to do is slowly start counting to 10 and say to yourself 'calm down.' This is when you can use your 1 + 3 + 10 formula for calming down."

2. **A = Ask** what signals the body is sending. Say, "Next, think how your body feels. Is your body signaling danger signs? Are you losing control? Use those signals to help you calm down."

3. **L = List** in your mind (or on a piece of paper) ways to stay in control. Ask students to consider, "What are your choices?" Brainstorm with students calming down techniques, such as walking away, doing relaxation exercises, taking three deep breaths, asking for help. Say, "Think of all your choices and then ask yourself, 'What would happen if I made that choice?'"

RT28a

RT28b

C	= Count
A	= Ask
L	= List
M	= Make

4. **M = Make** a plan for the best way to use self-control. Do it! Tell students, "Choose the best way to control yourself and then do it. Remember, if your plan doesn't work, you can always choose another one. That's what self-control is all about."

Provide students with a copy of the "Calming Down" skill builder. Ask them to put the form in their notebook.

Note: A complete Self-Control Plan (RT28b) is provided in the Worksheet Section located in the back of the book.

RT28b

This plan is to be used by individual students who need to practice the technique of staying calm. It can also be used following an "out of control" incident to help these students develop a plan for more responsible behavior the next time.

SELF-CONTROL PLEDGE RT 29

Purpose: To teach students to be accountable for their behavior by developing a plan to develop self-control and replace irresponsible actions.

Thought: *Nothing gives one person so much advantage over another as to remain always cool and unruffled under all circumstances.*—Thomas Jefferson

Vocabulary: Commitment, pledge, promise, resolution, covenant.

RT29

Materials:
- Self-Control Pledge (RT29); one per student.
- Pledge Shake (RT14); one copy enlarged poster size.

Procedure: Begin a class meeting by explaining to students that learning self-control will take some time and work. The important thing is for them to make a plan for a new behavior that will replace the behavior that could get them in trouble. Review the CALM steps (RT28a) with students and then distribute a copy of the Self-Control Pledge to each student. Ask them to take the time to prepare a plan for developing self-control. Say, "What will you do the next time your body sends you danger signals warning that you may be losing control? Write or draw what your best choice will be for self-control."

RT14

Review the Pledge Shake skill builder. If your students feel comfortable enough, ask them to share their plan with their partners and then "shake on the plan" as a sign of their commitment. Ask partners to be responsible for quietly reminding their classmates of their plan each day for a week.

CALM AND COOL AWARD   RT 30

Purpose: To recognize students for responsible behavior in using self-control.

Thought: *Anger is quieted by a gentle word, just as fire is quenched by water.*—Proverb

Materials:
- Calm and Cool Award (RT30); one per student.

For younger students:
- One 36" piece of yarn per award.

- Able Puppet (RT1b).

- Spinner Puppet (RT22a).

RT30

Procedure: For younger students, print multiple copies of the award on light-colored construction paper and cut out along the outside shape of the sign. Punch a hole in the top center of the sign about one inch from the edge. String a piece of yarn through the hole and tie a knot at the top of the yarn. Each time a teacher or student sees someone demonstrating self-control, he/she will present the student demonstrating the appropriate behavior with an award. *Also consider having the Able Puppet give the students their award.* For older students, make multiple copies of the Calm and Cool Award on light-colored paper. Distribute the grams to students who demonstrate self-control or the technique of calming down.

APOLOGIZING   RT 31

Purpose: To teach the skill of apologizing.

Thought: *It is much safer to reconcile an enemy than to conquer him; victory may deprive him of his poison, but reconciliation of his will*—Feltham.

Vocabulary: Apologizing, apology, sorry, regret, remorse, irresponsible, embarrassment, courage, interrupt, uninterrupted.

Materials:
- Apologizing (RT31); one per student and one enlarged poster size.

- *For younger students:* Able (RT1b) and Spinner (RT22a) Puppets.

RT31

Procedure: Gather students in a Class Meeting and say, "Sometimes we do things we later wish we hadn't. We say or do things we're sorry for and then we regret doing them." Explain that we still have choices. Say, "We could keep it inside us and not let the person know we're sorry or we could let the person know we're sorry and wish it had not happened." Ask students which response is responsible and which is not responsible. Say, "When we tell someone we're sorry it's called apologizing."

You might ask students to discuss a time they felt sorry and apologized, or describe how they felt after apologizing. Mention that "saying you're sorry often makes you feel better." Emphasize it's easy to avoid making apologies, but it takes courage to be responsible for apologizing. Say, "When you apologize you might feel embarrassed. It's not easy but it is the right thing to do." Explain that apologies can't erase what you've done but it may help change the person's opinion of you or make them less upset about the incident. Tell students sometimes the person may not accept your apology, but at least you can tell yourself you did the right thing and acted responsibly.

> *For younger students:* Use the Able and Spinner Puppets to role play the behavior of apologizing. Able apologizes to Spinner for ignoring him the first time he came to visit their galaxy by saying, "I'm sorry we didn't set out a welcome mat for you. I could have told you to come another time. I know it made you feel upset." Then he shakes the comet's hand. Spinner responds by saying, "I accept your apology."

Introduce the skill builder form entitled Apologizing and describe the five steps to making an apology by saying the following:

1. Ask yourself, "What did I do? Do I need to tell the person I'm sorry?"

2. Choose a time and place that's private to be with the person. It's best to apologize when you're alone and uninterrupted. Try to apologize as soon as you can. Waiting a long time often makes it more difficult.

3. Choose the best way to tell the person you're sorry. You could say you're sorry to the person or write a letter or even do something to try and make up for what happened. If you broke something, for example, you could try to fix it.

4. Be sincere and as calm as you can. Let the person know you're sorry, "I'm sorry," and then let the person know what you did that you regret. You might also tell them you know how they feel.

   "I'm sorry I broke your ruler. I didn't mean to."

   "I'm sorry I told Jenny the secret. I wish I hadn't. I know it made you feel upset."

5. If you feel comfortable, ask if there's anything you can do to make things better or let the person know what you plan to do to make things better. Remember, the person may or may not choose to accept your apology. That's okay. You made the right choice.

Role Playing: Students may practice the skill of apologizing in pairs, teams or groups. Below are a few role playing incidents in which to practice the skill. *For younger students, the Able Puppet can act out the behaviors (i.e., coming late to class, losing a borrowed pencil, interrupting the teacher, blurting out a secret someone told him).*

- You're late to your friend's party.
- You accidentally broke or lost something.
- You're late for class.
- You broke your neighbor's window with a baseball.
- You told someone a secret and the person who told you never to tell finds out.
- You interrupted someone's conversation.
- You accidentally stepped on someone's toe.
- You accidentally tore someone's jacket.
- You said something unkind and now regret it.
- You missed your friend's birthday.

Provide each student a copy of the Apologizing skill builder form to put in their Character Builder Notebook. Hang the poster-size copy on the wall for students to refer to.

RT31

RESPONSIBILITY PHONE CALL   RT 32

Purpose: To help students learn to take responsibility for misbehavior.

Thought: *He who makes excuses accuses himself.*—French Proverb

Materials:
- Responsibility Phone Call Script (RT32).
- For older students: 1:3:1 Repair Sheet (RT34d)

Procedure: Tell students the purpose of discipline at this school is for students to learn to take responsibility for their misbehavior. Ask students, if their behavior is unacceptable should the teacher or the misbehaving student be responsible for telling the parents? Confirm that the student and not the teacher will be responsible for calling the parent from school, explaining what the misbehavior was, and coming up with a plan for behaving appropriately.

RT32

Share the Responsibility Phone Call script with students and explain how the new phone policy will work. A misbehaving student will be given the Responsibility Phone Call Script to take to the office and phone home to explain the problem to his/her parents, to tell how the student was responsible, and to say what he/she will be do next time to remedy the problem. *Idea developed by Clyde Hill Elementary School, Bellevue, WA.*

BOOKS TO ENHANCE EMOTIONAL AWARENESS `RT 33`

Purpose: To help students explore their own emotions and thereby further develop self-understanding; to encourage the use of constructive ways to deal with feelings.

Thought: *The man who doesn't read good books has no advantage over the man who can't read them.*—Mark Twain

Materials: One or more books from the list below appropriate to grade level. Either read aloud or assign as independent reading. Many are particularly suitable for classroom discussions and as preparation or follow-up for the lessons in this section.

[P] Primary   [U] Upper

Alexander and the Terrible, Horrible, No Good, Very Bad Day by Judith Viorst (Atheneum, 1972). [P]

The Bear's House by Marilyn Sachs (Price, Stern & Sloan, 1986). The dark of night and a vivid imagination can make ordinary things seem scary. [P]

Do Bananas Chew Gum? by Jamie Gibson (Lothrop, Lee & Shepard, 1980). A boy deals with his learning disability. [U]

Do I Have to Go to School Today? Squib Measures Up by Larry Shles (Jalmar Press, 1989). [ALL]

The Do-Something Day by Joe Lasker (Scholastic, 1982). [P]

Feelings by Aliki (Greenwillow, 1984). [ALL]

Feelings Alphabet: An Album of Emotions from A to Z by Judy Lalli (Jalmar Press, 1984). [ALL]

The Gold Cadillac by Mildred D. Taylor (Dial, 1987). Deals with prejudice against blacks in the 1950s. [U]

How I Feel by J. Behrens (Children's Press, 1973). [P]

I Have Feelings by Terry Berger (Human Sciences, 1971). [U]

Immigrant Girl, Becky of Eldridge Street by Brett Harvey (Holiday, 1987). [U]

Molly's Pilgrim by Barbara Cohen (Lothrop, Lee & Shepard, 1983). Deals with ridicule and rejection by classmates. [P]

Nobody Listens to Andrew by Elizabeth Guilfoile (Scholastic, 1957). [P]

Rose Blanche by Roberto Innocenti (Creative Education, 1985). Story concerns the horror of the holocaust. [U]

The Shrinking of Treehorn by Florence Parry Heide (Holiday House, 1971). Concerns the issue of not being listened to. [P–U]

The Stone-Faced Boy by Paula Fox (Aladdin, 1968). Ridicule and rejection from classmates cause Gus to turn off his emotions and become "stone-faced." [U]

Today Was a Terrible Day by Patricia Reilly Giff (Puffin, 1980). A terrible, frustrating day is turned around for Ronald Morgan by a loving teacher. [P]

What I Like by Catherine and Laurence Anholt (G.P. Putnam's Sons, 1991). Rhymes, text, and illustrations describe a child's likes and dislikes which create individuality. [P]

Anger:

Boy Was I Mad! by Kathryn Hitte (Parents, 1969). [P]

Feeling Angry by Sylvia Root Tester (Children's Press, 1976). [P]

The Hating Book by Charlotte Zolotow (Harper & Row, 1969). [P]

I Was So Mad! by Norma Simon (Albert Whitman, 1974). [P]

The Quarreling Book by Charlotte Zolotow (Harper & Row, 1963). [P]

Sometimes I Get Angry by J.W. Watson (Golden, 1971). [P]

Temper Tantrum Book by Edna M. Preston (Viking, 1969). [P]

Where the Wild Things Are by Maurice Sendak (Harper & Row, 1963). [P]

"Liberty means responsibility. That is why most men dread it."
—MAXIMS FOR REVOLUTIONISTS

 **5**

Becoming a
Responsible Learner

CHARACTER BUILDER STEP #4:

- Develop Responsibilities as a Learner

KEY OBJECTIVES:

- Following Through

- Forming Study Buddy Partnerships

- Tracking Student Progress

- Modeling Responsibility

- Learning Accountability

5

Becoming a
Responsible Learner

Responsibility for learning belongs to the student, regardless of age.
—ROBERT MARTIN

All teachers dream of students who are self-directed and responsible. These are the kind of students who start projects—and then finish on their own. When these students make a mistake they acknowledge their error and don't shove the blame onto someone else: they take ownership for the error and admit it. And, when these students complete an assignment (and it's almost always on time), they don't need "scratch and sniff" stickers to affirm their efforts. They do appreciate our praise and encouraging statements, but they don't need to rely on external rewards as motivators. They use themselves to regulate their performance. In short, they are "internally empowered" instead of "externally controlled." These students have acquired what psychologists call "an internal locus of control," that is, they recognize they have responsibility as well as control over their own actions.

Anything we can do that helps students become more self-disciplined and responsible will help increase their chances of success in school as well as life. An important first step towards this journey is to teach students the skills to help them become more accountable for their own learning. Educational psychologist, Raymond Wlodkowski, affirms just how critical enhancing traits of self-direction are to our students' school success. He states that "90 percent [of learning] is self-directed. No one is going to sit next to our children the rest of their lives and help them to study, to do quality work, to think, and to make the extra effort that develops excellent skills. That is a job only the self can accomplish, and the self needs practice to make such habits of self-regulation automatic responses."

Raymond J. Wlodkowski and Judith H. Jaynes. *Eager to Learn: Helping Children Become Motivated and Love Learning*. (San Francisco: Jossey-Bass Publishers, 1991).

CHARACTER BUILDER STEP #4

Develop Responsibilities as a Learner

Responsibility means accountability. It's a significant learning concept for today's students to acquire. After all, for optimum motivation to ever evolve, students must recognize that responsibility for learning rests on their shoulders. This final section offers practical ways for students to monitor and be responsible for their own assignments. The development of this ability will move us one step further from continually reminding students to be responsible and one step closer to helping them be accountable for their own behavior.

Enhancing the trait of self-responsibility in students obviously takes time. It also needs to be consistently reinforced. A strong suggestion, therefore, is to choose any of the activities in the section, and then have your students work on the same task for at least 21 days. Social learning theories state that change takes a minimum of three weeks. Many of these techniques can become ongoing study organizers that can be used throughout the school year. You may even want to set aside a brief time each day for students to "organize their responsibilities" using one of the activities.

Finally, consider using the cooperative structure described in the section called Study Buddies. Many teachers give me rave reviews on how the activity not only improved their students' social skills and feelings of belonging but also greatly enhanced their accountability as learners. Each day for three minutes the teachers asked their students to make sure their assigned Study Buddy had written down their learning assignments correctly and completed all assigned tasks "responsibly." Those three minutes, the teachers said, had a dramatic impact on their students' level of responsibility: they not only learned organization skills that helped them to be accountable for their own tasks but they also began to feel responsible for their partner's learning. True responsibility involves doing what's best not only for yourself but also for others. The fourth Character Builder step shows you the way.

Activities to Develop Learner Responsibilities		

The activities listed below are taken from the *Esteem Builders* series written by Dr. Michele Borba.

Code	Activity	Page
Esteem Builder Activities		
C20	Work Contract	303
C19	Academic Progress Charts	281
C21	Reading Garden	282
C22	Ollie Owl Book Report	282

Esteem Builders

Home Esteem Builders

*For more information about these books, call Jalmar Press at 800/662-9662. They can be purchased individually or in a kit.

STUDY BUDDIES

Study Buddies is a cooperative learning structure in which the teacher assigns each student a partner. The Buddy is simply another student in the classroom. The length of time students remain as partners is optional: many teachers change student partnerships weekly, others monthly, and for some teachers the relationship continues for the semester or even the year. The most important advice is to make the structure work for you.

Study Buddies can be an invaluable way to increase students' learning responsibilities not only for themselves but also for one another. Teachers report that keeping the same two students together for even a week can be a valuable esteem enhancer for partners. By the end of the week, after repeatedly sharing activities, the pairs generally are closer because the process has given them the opportunity to find out about one another. As a result, a "support" network has developed between the two students.

Students pair with partners for a variety of activities. No activity needs to be longer than three minutes in length. Pairing activities might include:

1. Direction Agreement. Students turn to their partners, and as quickly as they can, the two must agree on what the directions to the assignment are before they begin to work on the task alone.

2. Problem Management. Any time students have a problem that they cannot solve, before asking the teacher they must first ask their partners if they can solve it. Many teachers make a rule that before students ask the teacher a question, they must first, "Ask your Study Buddy."

3. Homework Review. Any homework assignment can become a "three-minute Study Buddy review." For instance, suppose the homework assignment last night was to read a lengthy section in their books. In three minutes, students are to find their partners and discuss three main points they remember reading.

"You can't escape the responsibility of tomorrow by evading it today."

—Abraham Lincoln

4. *Study Partners.* Partners can help one another prepare for tests, projects or presentations. The simplest way to begin Study Partners is to ask each team to give one another a "one-minute quiz" on any content required for memorization (i.e. spelling words, vocabulary terms, math facts, geographic locations).

5. *Written Language.* Students are asked to write an essay on an assigned topic. Before beginning, students quickly turn to their Study Buddies and tell them what they plan to write about. The partners can suggest one idea to consider. Now students begin to write.

6. *Book Buddy.* Students are asked to find one page in their reading books that they enjoy. They now turn to their partners and take turns reading the page aloud.

7. *Affirmations.* Study Buddies can also be a valuable way to help create "human connections" for students at the school site. The possibilities for connections are endless. One simple approach is to ask Study Buddies to call any partners who are absent and tell them they are missed, or design a get-well card and have it signed by other classmates. Study Buddies can also be the first persons each day to issue a classroom greeting. "Hi, I'm glad you're here" can be a powerful way to start a day.

> "A new position of responsibility will usually show a man to be a far stronger creature than was supposed."
> —William James

Forming Study Buddy Partnerships

There is no right or wrong way to divide students into partnerships. Many teachers find that randomly pairing students is the simplest technique. Do keep in mind this critical premise: Study Buddy groups will be more successful if students feel comfortable with each other. You may need to do extra planning to develop a structure for students low in self-esteem and lacking in social skills.

A suggestion from Jeanne Gibbs in her Tribes' program is to ask each student to print the name of six other classmates he/she would like to have as a partner. Collect the cards and then begin to form Study Buddy combinations by first looking to see if any of the "higher risk" students you've identified appear on the list of any other students. Pair these students first.

Safer Partners for At-Risk Students

The following is a list of the types of students who are "safer" partners for students with low esteem.

- *Less confident student.* A quiet, more reserved student is often a better choice as a partner for a student with low security than a more confident, verbal partner.

- *Same sex.* A partner of the same sex can be less-threatening than a partner of the opposite sex (particularly to a pre-adolescent student).

- *More compassionate.* A student with a more merciful heart is often more empathetic towards a student with lower skills and esteem. Do recognize, though, that a more compassionate student is frequently chosen for the role of "merciful partner," so please don't abuse their kind heart by always pairing them with an at-risk partner.

- *You.* In some cases, you may have to be this student's partner for a while until they learn the skills for working with others. In the meantime, consider having the student become a cross-age tutor for awhile. If the student is in the third grade, for instance, ask him/her to tutor a first-grade student for a brief time each day. Research finds that students often feel threatened when paired with a peer but are much more secure trying their new skills with a younger student. After awhile, the student will transfer the newly-learned social skill practiced with the younger student to his/her own peers.

Study Buddy Activities

The activities listed below are taken from the *Esteem Builders* series written by Dr. Michele Borba.

Esteem Builders

Code	Activity	Page

Esteem Builder Activities to provide study buddies with opportunities to learn more about each other.

S21	Student Interview	62
A2	Common Points	166
A3	Getting to Know You Wheel	166
A4	Paired Name Collage	167

STUDY BUDDIES

RT 34a

Purpose: To provide opportunities for students to encourage and support one another's learning responsibilities.

Thought: *By helping somebody climb a mountain of problems, I solve some of mine too.*—Anonymous

RT34a   RT34b

Materials:

- Study Buddies (RT34a); one per student and one printed poster-size to hang in the classroom.

- *For older students:* Study Buddy Facts (RT34b); one per student.

- *For younger students:* My Study Buddy (RT34c); one per student. Ink pads, paper towels and magnifying glasses for taking one another's fingerprints (optional).

- Able (RP1) and Spinner (RP7) puppets.

Literature:

From Far Away by Robert Munsch (Annick Press, 1995). A girl who moves from Beirut to Canada must deal not only with vast cultural differences but feelings of alienation. The story begins with the character writing a letter to her Reading Buddy, which makes it a perfect link to the Study Buddy activity. The book is based on an actual series of letters between a seven-year old girl and the author. [Primary Students]

Procedure: Divide students into assigned Study Buddies (see "Forming Study Buddy Partnerships" on page 94). Ideally, the partners' desks are side by side, close enough so paired activities take a minimum of time and noise. Explain that Study Buddies is a way for students to help one another become more responsible for their own learning. Provide students with a copy of Study Buddies (RT34a) and review rules for the Class Meeting. Tell students these will be the same responsibilities students have for one another whenever they meet as Study Buddies.

Briefly describe the kinds of responsibilities Study Buddies can have for one another. Explain the first responsibility is for Study Buddies to write each other's phone numbers on the Study Buddy fact sheet. Emphasize that the sheet should be stored in a safe location. Any students who are absent or unsure of the work that has been assigned in the classroom are responsible for calling their Study Buddy to clarify the assignment. They are also responsible for calling Study Buddies who are absent to find out how they're feeling and to tell them what they missed at school. Tell students they could make a get-well card for their partner and have classmates sign it to give to the Study Partner when they return. Refer to the Study Buddy poster to discuss other responsibilities Study Buddies could have for one another.

The Study Buddy Nightmare

For younger students, tell a story about Able and Spinner who became Study Buddies at the Galaxy School. Use the puppets when telling the story. Say, "Able, being the shooting star he is, was a responsible learner. He came to school on time, did all his homework, and tried to improve on each assignment he turned in. Spinner, on the other hand, was everybody's Study Buddy nightmare. He came to class only when he happened to be in the galaxy and he never knew what the assignment was.

"Out of concern for his buddy, Able sent Spinner a get-well card every time the comet was absent. Messages like 'We miss you' and 'Come back soon' made Spinner wish he could see his classmates again. When the comet finally showed up for school,

Able gave him a big smile and a folder filled with all of the assignments Spinner had missed. The folder was two inches thick. The comet felt his life spinning out of control again; he just knew he could never catch up now. His first thought was to run away and just go back to aimlessly roaming the universe, but Able immediately offered to help him out, saying, 'Look through the assignments and I'll explain what each one is about and what you need to do to complete it.' Reluctantly, Spinner looked at the first assignment: Draw two pictures, one of yourself being 'responsible' and one of yourself being 'not responsible.'

"'Responsible means doing what's right,' Able explained. 'That's easy enough,' Spinner thought. 'I can draw one picture of me turning in a homework assignment and another picture of me sleeping in late on a weekday.' 'Good job!' Able said when the comet had finished drawing two pictures of himself. Then he told Spinner specifically what he liked about the picture. 'I like the bright colors on your tail.' Able also told the comet what he could do to improve next time. 'You could draw a straighter line right here,' Able said, pointing to the bedframe, 'and stay inside the lines.' Then he encouraged his Study Buddy until they had completed all the assignments Spinner had missed.

"With Able's help, Spinner got his homework under control. He started showing up for school every day knowing that someone would explain the assignment to him if he didn't understand it. And when Able was out sick, Spinner would do the same for him. The two Study Buddies soon became good friends."

> "Life has no meaning except in terms of responsibility."
> —Reinhold Nieburh

Provide older students with a copy of Study Buddy Facts and explain that they have ten minutes (or longer) to get to know about each other. Completed forms should be kept in the front of students' binders or backpacks so that the information about their partner is available not only at school but at home.

Provide younger students with a copy of My Study Buddy and begin by discussing the interview questions. Then show the children how to fingerprint themselves by pressing their finger onto an ink pad and then onto a sheet of scratch paper. Provide paper towels so the children can wipe off the ink that remains on their fingers following the fingerprinting activity. You may wish to provide magnifying glasses and encourage the children to examine their fingerprints more closely. Have the children compare their fingerprints, noting differences and similarities.

Variation: Copy students' completed Study Buddy and My Study Buddy fact sheets and compile them alphabetically by students' last names into a folder called "Class Directory." The directory can be used by all students to locate their classmates' interests, areas of "expertise," and phone numbers.

STUDY BUDDY CENTER RT 35

Purpose: To provide opportunities for Study Buddies to support each other and help their absent partner with missed assignments.

Thought: *None is so great that he needs no help, and none is so small that he cannot give it.*—King Solomon

Literature:

Sam Who Never Forgets by Eve Rice (New York: Greenwillow Books, 1977). Here's a delightful tale of a young child whose parent gives him the responsibility of remembering to bring home a few items. The tale is a great catalyst for a discussion about the benefits of making lists so we don't forget. [Primary Students]

Materials: Set up a box or table display for students to use with materials such as marking pens, scissors, colored pencils, crayons, stickers, stamp pads and stamps, yarn, hole-punch, stars, paste or glue, staplers, construction paper and a computer. Place the display in an accessible location.

Procedure: Tell students that an important part of being a good Study Buddy is to help their partners make up missed assignments. Explain that if their partners are absent, students should design a folder at the Study Buddy Center to file all assignments the partners have missed. Encourage students to design a "get well" or "we missed you" message on the front of the folder and hand it to their partners when they return. Explain that the Study Buddy Center is available to design cards, posters or certificates to support one another as occasions arise.

LEARNER RESPONSIBILITIES LOG RT 36

Purpose: To increase students' responsibility in keeping track of their individual school assignments.

Thoughts:

- *If I plan to learn, I must learn to plan.*—Ancient Proverb

- *Do every act of your life as if it were your last.*—Marcus Aurelius

- *Small opportunities are often the beginnings of great enterprises.*—Demosthenes

- *I can give you a six-word formula for success: Think things through—then follow through.*—Edward Rickenbacker

Literature:

Mr. Meant-To by anonymous author. The following short poem, entitled "Mr. Meant-To", is wonderful to use with older students as a discussion tool for the subjects of procrastination and self-responsibility. You may wish to write the words to the poem on a chart and hang it in a visible location, or have students copy the poem in their Character Builder Notebook.

Mr. Meant-To

Mr. Meant-To has a comrade,
And his name is Didn't-Do.
Have you ever chanced to meet them?
Have they ever called on you?
These two fellows live together
In the House of Never Win,
And I'm told that it is haunted
By the ghost of Might-Have-Been.

— Anonymous

Materials: Learner Responsibilities Log; (RT36) one for every student each week.

Procedure: Emphasize that success in school as well as in all areas of life is not a matter of "luck" but comes about by planning. Explain that each week students are to write down their assignments on the form. Completed assignments are then checked off in the right-hand column. Tell them that this is one way to be "answerable" for their learning.

Set a rule that any time students are unsure of an assignment, they are to simply ask their Study Buddies for clarification. Emphasize that when students help one another learn responsibility there are no excuses for not knowing an assignment. Prior to dismissal, Study Buddies can take a few minutes each day to confirm learning assignments and check each other's Learning Responsibilities Log.

For Younger Students: Younger students can keep track of their work responsibilities in a weekly folder. To make each folder:

1. Fold an 12" × 18" piece of construction paper in half so the folder is now 9" × 12". Take another 12" × 18" paper and fold it in half the long way. It is now 6" × 18".

2. Slip the long piece along the bottom of the folder so the folded edge is along the bottom edge. Staple the two pages together along the edges. The inside of the folder will have two stapled pockets. One pocket can be designated for "work to do" and the other pocket can be used to store "completed work."

3. A weekly progress report can be stapled on the front of the folder to enhance communication between parents and the teacher.

> "And so, my fellow Americans, ask not what your country can do for you: ask what you can do for your country."
>
> — John F. Kennedy

Tracking Student Progress

Keeping a portfolio can be a valuable technique to strengthen students' accountability for their learning. Not only are students responsible for collecting work samples that demonstrate learning competencies but they are able to see evidence of their learning progress. Making the portfolio process manageable is critical to their success.

The first step is for you to choose a portfolio that is convenient to store and easily accessible to both you and your students. Some teachers keep them in a large box on the floor or a special shelf in a bottom drawer of a file cabinet. The least effective storage location is students' desks since, too often, items are misplaced or damaged.

Next, develop a schedule for having students collect work samples. Is it once a week on Friday? Everyday at 2:30? Monday morning at 8:00 a.m.? Set a time and then consistently ask students to store a sample of their best learning. Remember to tell students exactly what you expect to be collected: the types of categories as well as the number of items.

Finally, think about what you want students to learn from their portfolios. Think about how they—and you—will evaluate their learning progress and develop the skills of self-responsibility. You need not limit portfolio collections to only "best work" samples. Consider using the concept of "gain" as a criteria.

The definition of success is a four letter word spelled: G - A - I - N.
—Webster's Dictionary

G – Growth. A new learning discovery or breakthrough.
A – Achievement. A best paper; an outstanding effort.
I – Improvement. An assignment that shows progress; "Where I was . . . where I am now . . . I'm getting better!"
N – Narrative. A written account from the student or teacher (or both) as to what was learned.

STUDENT PORTFOLIOS   RT 37

Purpose: To enhance students' responsibilities as learners by tracking their progress.

Thought: *Image is the great instrument of instruction.*—John Dewey

Literature:
When I Was Little by Jamie Lee Curtis (Harper Collins, 1993). This is a delightful four-year-old's memoir of her new-found capabilities. The repetitive refrain, "When I was little I . . .

but now I . . .," is wonderful to use with younger students as they refer to beginning portfolio collections and then see evidence of their learning as compared to later selections.

Materials: There are dozens of ways for students to keep track of their learning performance. Several of the most manageable devices are described below. The key is to find a simple portfolio technique that is beneficial for the students and works well for you.

Procedure: Begin by selecting a portfolio technique (from below or one you invented yourself) and then consistently (at least once a week!) ask students to collect evidence of their learning "gains" to store in their portfolio. Emphatically emphasize the rule: "Students' portfolios may not be looked at without their owner's permission."

- *Tape Recordings.* Students record their learning progress in a particular academic area on a tape cassette. Learning recordings include: read-alouds from favorite books, auditory memories, nursery rhymes, interviews with peers, vocabulary terms, and oral readings of essays, poems or other material written by the students. Another suggestion is for students to tape a summary of what they learned for the week.

- *Cereal Boxes.* I learned this technique from a middle school language arts teacher and I've yet to see a simpler portfolio. She asked each student to bring in an empty cereal box that "somehow represented them" (which means some kids will be bringing in "Wheaties" and others "Fruit Loops," but that's the fun of it!) Now, carefully remove the top of the box. Ask students to print their names on a gummed label and attach it to the side of the box. Each week (or day) students select papers depicting progress in a particular subject, then date and file them in the box. The teacher stores the boxes on a shelf.

- *Five-Minute Portfolio.* At the beginning of the year, set a goal each student can work towards. Options include: draw a person, write your name, write a sentence using proper punctuation, or write a paragraph. The list is endless. Simply adapt the activity to your students' needs. Provide each student with a manila folder. Each Friday (or any other day) bring out a timer and set it for an appropriate time (the shorter the better). Students are to do the task (i.e. write one paragraph on any topic) before the timer goes off. At the stroke of the bell, the task stops, is dated, and compared to the previous week's task and finally stored in the appropriate manila folder.

- *Mastery Boxes.* Consider using this devise for recording the mastery of new learning facts, such as reading words, spelling words, vocabulary terms, math facts or any key terms. Each student brings a shoebox from home and prepares alphabetical dividers from tagboard. Newly-mastered facts are printed on cards (sized to fit the shoe boxes) and filed in the appropriate alphabetical section.

- *GAIN Notebooks.* Students divide spiral-bound notebooks into categories such as Gains, Achievements, Improvements and Narratives. Assignments depicting each of the four categories (or others) are filed in the appropriate sections.

- *Favorite Work Folder.* Younger students decorate and fold in half lengthwise a 14"
  × 20" piece of cardstock-weight paper. Punch several evenly-spaced holes on both
  short sides of the folded paper. Ask students to use an overcast stitch and sew the
  folder sides together with cord or yarn (or simply staple the sides of the folder
  together). Invite students to print a cover title such as, "My Favorite Work Folder,"
  and their names on the folders (or print this for them). Decorate a box in which to
  store the Favorite Work Folders. When any students do particularly good work or
  seem to enjoy a project more than usual, ask if they would like to save the paper.
  Older students may use a simple manila folder to collect outstanding assignments.

- *Letter.* Ask students to look through their portfolio and then write a letter (to
  themselves, teacher, study buddy, or parent) describing their learning progress.
  The letter is usually stored as the first item in the portfolio.

- *Video Portfolio.* If you're fortunate enough to have video equipment, consider having
  students keep a video portfolio of their progress in a particular subject area. A
  student camera crew can periodically interview students, or record learning progress
  in action. Projects, reports and stories all lend themselves well to videos. A student
  can read his/her report while another student videotapes him/her. Students can also
  be interviewed periodically, for example, "What's one thing you learned this week?"

STUDY BUDDY PORTFOLIO EVALUATION RT 38

Purpose: To enhance students' awareness of their learning responsibilities by working in
partnerships to monitor their progress.

Thought: *"So wherever I am, there's always Pooh, there's always Pooh and me. "What
would I do," I said to Pooh, "if it wasn't for you?" and Pooh said, "True! It isn't much fun for
one, but two can stick together," says Pooh.*—A. A. Milne

Materials: Study Buddy Portfolio Evaluation (RT38); one copy for each Study Buddy team.
Any selection from the student's portfolio.

Procedure: Ask each student to choose one selection from their portfolio depicting their
"best work." Now ask students to join their Study Buddy, and take turns evaluating one
another's selection by completing the three criteria on the Study Buddy Portfolio Evaluation.

Adaptation For Younger Children: Provide each student with a piece of newsprint paper
folded in half. Draw a "happy face" on the left side and a face with no mouth on the other.
Students choose a favorite selection from their Favorite Work Folder. Working with their
Study Buddy, students discuss the "things they like about the work" on the left side. Positive attributes may be drawn or dictated on the left side of the paper. Explain that the second face has no expression (the face is not happy or sad) because the face knows there are

a few things that might make the selection even better. Say: "If there was one thing you might have done that would turn the face into a happy face what would it be?" Students dictate these ideas on the right side of the paper.

RESPONSIBILITY PLEDGE `RT 39`

Purpose: To instill in students the need to take responsibility for setting expectations and then following through.

Thought: *Procrastination is the thief of time.*—Edward Young

Materials:
- Pledge Shake (RT14); one copy enlarged poster size.

Literature: *Frog Medicine* by Mark Teague (Scholastic, 1991).

Procedure: In a Class Meeting, share with students the book, *Frog Medicine,* to set the tone for being responsible for homework and not procrastinating (or putting things off). Discuss the concept of "carrying out responsibilities" and explain how it often involves good organization.

Ask students to choose one "learning" responsibility that could help them be more successful. This might be a rule on the Responsibility Covenant they have problems following, a study skill, or even a social skill that's getting in the way of their relationships. Students can "whip" around the Class Meeting circle briefly describing their choices.

Distribute a copy of the Pledge Shake to each student. Working with their Study Buddy (or alone), students write down their pledge. Then they briefly share a learning goal with their partners and show their commitment to improving with the Pledge Shake. At the end of each day, students again share with their partners, summarizing how successful they were with their goal.

RESPONSIBILITY STEPS `RT 40`

Purpose: To enhance students' awareness of their learning responsibilities by setting a daily goal.

Materials:
- Responsibility Steps (RT40); one per student.
- *For younger children:* Able (RP1) and Spinner (RP7) Puppets.

RT40

Thought: *Few things help an individual more than to place responsibility upon him, and to let him know that you trust him.*—Booker T. Washington

Procedure: Ask students: "What are things you can do to be responsible for your school work?" List these ideas on a chart or blackboard and keep the list visible for the next step in the activity. Next, ask students to reflect on what they will do to personally be responsible for their learning. Ask students to write or draw the learning goal on their form and then add the first step they'll take to get started.

You may wish to set aside a few minutes each day for students to focus on what they will do to be accountable that day for their school work. The activity can be extended to a Study Buddy task by asking students to say their goal and then ask their partners to quietly remind them one time during the day of what they said they want to accomplish.

Able Shares Good Learning Pointers

For younger children: Begin by drawing a big star on the blackboard as Able offers Spinner a few "pointers" on how to succeed in school. Spinner has not been getting good grades on his assignments. He admits he rushes through his homework so he can play Spin the Tail on the Comet with his friends. He asks his Study Buddy how he can improve. On each point of the star, write in one of Able's suggestions…work quietly, write down the assignment, do your best every time, check your paper over before you turn it in, learn from your mistakes.

Follow-up Activity: Students make their own large star from construction paper and then draw or write a point they will remember to help them be a STAR (Success Through Acting Responsibly). The star can be lightly brushed with glue and sprinkled with glitter.

EXCUSE BUSTERS RT 41

Purpose: To teach students that being responsible means not making excuses but being accountable.

Thought: *Win without boasting. Lose without excuse.*—Albert Payson Terhune
NO EXCUSES!

Literature: *John Patrick Norman McHennessy: The Boy Who Was Always Late* by John Burningham (Crown Publishers, 1987). A teacher gives out harsh consequences for John

Patrick Norman McHennessy's tardiness and then regrets his decision to disbelieve a student's outlandish excuses for being tardy. Consider using this book to discuss the consequences of breaking rules (All).

Materials:

- 12" × 18" light-colored construction paper or newsprint, colored markers and/or crayons; per each Study Buddy team.

- *For younger students:* a balloon and a pin.

Procedure: Gather students together for a Class Meeting. Write the word "accountable" on the blackboard or chart paper. Ask students to explain the meaning. Responses include: responsible, answerable, liable, the ability to answer for the consequences of our own choices and actions. Discuss how accountable people do not make excuses. They accept the responsibility for their behaviors. You might ask students to describe an excuse they or someone else has used.

For younger students: Say, "Spinner had lots of excuses for why he couldn't get his homework in on time. The comet would say things like the assignment had burnt up when he re-entered his home atmosphere or it was just too hard for a comet with a small head like his to grasp. But Able, his Study Buddy, wouldn't accept any excuses." Blow up a balloon and use a pin to pop it as Able says, "No excuses. You are responsible to do your own work." Explain that what Able told Spinner is called an 'Excuse Buster.'

For all ages: Tell students one way to get rid of excuses is to stamp them out. Draw on the board or chart paper the universal sign for "stamp out" or "not acceptable" (a large red or black circle with a line slashed diagonally through the circle from left to right). Write the words "No Excuses" in the middle of the circle. Tell students they now are to work with their Study Buddy to make their own Excuse Buster signs. Provide paper and pens to each team and explain they are to create their own sign for No Excuses. Somewhere on the sign the teams must include these three items:

1. a symbol that excuses are not acceptable,

2. the definition of responsibility, and

3. a few favorite excuses for not turning in work (list or draw) that are no longer acceptable in the classroom.

Hang up the finished signs around the room to remind students they are accountable for their work.

MODELS OF RESPONSIBILITY RT 42

Purpose: To help students analyze behaviors of responsibility in real individuals.

Thought: Ralph Waldo Emerson visited Henry David Thoreau in jail where Thoreau was serving a sentence for not paying his taxes. Emerson said, "What in heaven's name are you doing in jail?" Thoreau said, "What are you doing out of it?"

Materials:

- *For Younger Students:* Responsibility Report form (RT42a).

- *For Older Students:* Team Responsibility Report form (RT42b); Responsibility Projects (RT42c); and Responsibility Models (RT42d). One per student.

- Favorite children's literature selections that describe responsible individuals (or events). (See RT44, see pages 108–111.)

- Chart paper and pen (optional).

Procedure: Share a story of Harriet Tubman with students (or any other famous individual whose actions depict the theme of responsibility) and discuss why she is a "model of responsibility." You might wish to place her name with a brief phrase describing her responsible behavior on a chart labeled "Responsible Characters." (See Responsibility Models RT42d for more characters.)

Create a list of other historical or fictional characters whose behavior demonstrates responsibility. Now assign students (in teams or individually) to report on the life of a responsible character. Older students can work as a team and present their findings on responsibility to the class as a rap, chant, song, poetry reading, choral reading, skit, video or puppet presentation. (See Responsibility Projects RT42c for more ideas.) Younger students can write a simple sentence, draw a picture, or give a one-minute speech on the character.

Responsible Character Day. Students dress up as the responsible character and report in "first person" to the class on "how they acted responsibly."

Models of Responsibility

- Harriet Tubman
- Henry David Thoreau
- Patrick Henry
- Abraham Lincoln
- Dred Scott
- Martin Luther King, Jr.

- Albert Schweitzer
- Rosa Parks
- John Muir
- Susan B. Anthony
- Colin Powell
- Benjamin Franklin

- Cesar Chavez
- Winston Churchill
- Fredrick Douglas
- John Adams
- James Madison

"Ability will enable a man to get to the top, but it takes character to keep him there."

—Anonymous

Harriet Tubman: A Model of Social Responsibility

Born into slavery, young Harriet Tubman knew only work and hunger. Escape seemed impossible—certainly dangerous. Yet Harriet was strong-willed and courageous. "Some day," she said, "I'm going to be free."

When finally she did escape to the south, by the secret route called the Underground Railroad, Harriet didn't forget her people. Again and again, Harriet Tubman demonstrated responsibility for others by risking her life hundreds of times to lead Southern slaves on the same secret, dangerous journey to freedom.

- *The Story of Harriet Tubman: Freedom Train* by Dorothy Sterling (Scholastic, 1954). [Reading Level: 5th grade]

- *The Story of Harriet Tubman: Conductor of the Underground Railroad* by Kate McMullan (Dell, 1991). [Reading Level: 3.2]

- *Go Free or Die: A Story About Harriet Tubman* by Jeri Ferris (Carolrhoda Books, 1988). [Reading Level: 3.5]

- *Many Thousands Gone: African Americans from Slavery to Freedom* by Virginia Hamilton (Alfred A. Knopf, 1993). [ALL]

RESPONSIBILITY IN THE REAL WORLD   RT 43

Purpose: To encourage students to reflect on issues of responsibility in the real world.

Thought: *Corporations have a responsibility to make a positive contribution to the world.* —An Wang, founder of Wang Laboratories

Materials: Any bulletin board space such as a large piece of poster board, tagboard, cloth or bulletin board, push pins, construction paper cut-out letters or marking pen.

Procedure: Set aside a space for the activity and print a large caption: "Responsibility in the World." Emphasize to students that "responsibility" is a subject that is addressed everyday in the world. Cut out a few newspaper articles dealing with the subject and attach them to the board. Now encourage students to find additional articles addressing responsibility and add them to the board.

Follow-up ideas:
- *News Reports on Responsibility.* Assign a few students each day to report to the class on an issue related to real responsibility.

- *Responsibility Notebooks.* Ask students to cut and paste newspaper articles dealing with the theme of responsibility onto pages in their Responsibility Notebooks. After reading and reflecting on the article, students write about how the article addresses the theme.

- *Responsibility Debates.* Form student debate teams of two to four students and give each team a pro or con status. Assign teams a current news article, historical event, or literary character that in some way addresses the theme of responsibility and hold a class debate.

Topics for Responsibility Debates:

- *The Boston Tea Party.* Are the patriots responsible for the damage they caused during the rebellion?

- *The Stripping of Land from Native Americans.* Is the United States government responsible for compensating Native Americans for taking their land?

- *The Tobacco Industry vs. the Consumer.* If the tobacco industry was aware of research substantiating tobacco as a possible cause of cancer, is the industry responsible for reporting these findings to the public?

- *The United States Government vs. Japanese Americans.* Should Japanese Americans be compensated for being interned on American soil during World War II? Is the United States Government responsible for the Japanese Americans' emotional and financial losses?

- *From Literature:* Is the Little Red Hen in the fable responsible for feeding the other animals in the barnyard when they did not help her with the work?

- *Television ratings.* Should the television industry assume responsibility for making parents aware of the violent content and inappropriate language of certain television shows by assigning ratings?

> "Respon-
> sibility:
> A detach-
> able
> burden
> easily
> shifted to
> shoulders
> of God,
> Fate,
> Fortune,
> Luck, or
> one's
> neighbors."
> —Ambrose
> Pierce

CHILDREN'S LITERATURE ON RESPONSIBILITY   RT 44

Purpose: To gain awareness of the Character Builder trait of responsibility through children's literature.

Thought: *There is more treasure in books than in all the pirates loot on Treasure Island ... and the best of all, you can enjoy these riches every day of your life.*—Walt Disney

Materials: One or more books from the list below appropriate to grade level. Either read aloud or assign as independent reading.

Note: Although many of these books are listed as "Primary," most should be considered as "Everyone's Books." The concepts of responsibility and accountability contained in these texts are valuable for any age.

Primary Level:

A Children's Chorus by UNICEF (E.P. Dutton, 1989). This book celebrates the 30th anniversary of the Declaration of the Rights of the Child, unanimously adopted by the General Assembly of the United Nations in 1959. This landmark bill asserted ten fundamental rights for every child, including the right to adequate food, to safe shelter, to an education, and to a loving family. Each right is beautifully illustrated. The book can be a wonderful catalyst for a discussion of "rights" and "rules." (All ages.)

Be The Best You Can Be by Kirby Puckett (Minneapolis: Waldman House Press, 1993). The autobiography of baseball great, Kirby Puckett, is perfectly told in pictures. Puckett describes to his readers the expectations he set for himself and how they helped him succeed. This book is a must for all ages.

Elbert's Bad Word by Audrey Wood (Harcourt Brace Jovanovich, 1988). After shocking the elegant garden party by using a bad word, Elbert learns some acceptable substitutes from a helpful wizard. Use this book to enhance classroom discussions regarding the need to recognize how words as well as deeds can enhance or hinder responsible behavior.

Frog Medicine by Mark Teague (Scholastic, 1991). Elmo is given a book report assignment by his teacher and decides to wait until the last minute not only to begin the report but to choose the book. This is the perfect book to instill the need for not procrastinating and taking responsibility for your behavior.

Knots on a Counting Rope by Bill Martin, Jr. and John Archambault (Henry Holt and Company, 1987). Here is a wonderful tale of a grandfather who reminisces with his Indian grandson about his life and how he's successfully faced his greatest challenge—blindness. The grandfather tells his story around the campfire using the traditional "counting rope," a long strip of rope used by the storyteller. Key story points are emphasized by tying a knot in the rope.

John Patrick Norman McHennessy—The Boy Who Was Always Late by John Burningham (Crown Publishers, Inc. 1987). A teacher gives out harsh consequences when John Patrick Norman McHennessy is tardy and then regrets his decision to disbelieve a student's outlandish excuses for being late. Consider using this book to discuss the consequences of breaking rules. (All ages.)

From Far Away by Robert Munsch (Annick Press, 1995). A girl moves from Beirut to North America and must deal not only with vast cultural differences but feelings of alienation. The story begins with the character writing a letter to her Reading Buddy, making this book a perfect link to the Study Buddy activity. The book is based on an actual series of letters between a seven-year old girl and the author.

Miss Nelson Is Missing! by James Marshall and Harry Allard (Scholastic, 1977). This book is a gold mine (and a student favorite). A classroom gets out-of-hand and a teacher decides to get back control in a most ingenious way. Use it to begin a discussion of "What can we do in this classroom to maintain control?"

"One can acquire everything in solitude—except character."

—Henri Beyle

Never Spit on Your Shoes by Denys Cazet (Orchard Books, 1990). First-grader Arnie tells his mother about his first tiring day of first grade. He recounts such important incidents as sitting around in a circle and reading a chart of important classroom rules such as "Never spit on your shoes." Many teachers use this book as a catalyst to creating a rule chart for the classroom.

Officer Buckle and Gloria by Peggy Rathmann (G.P. Putnam's Sons, 1995). This Caldecott Medal winner for 1995 is ideal as a classroom tool for discussing "What rules do we need to feel or be safe?" The text describes the children at Napville Elementary School who always ignore Officer Buckle's safety tips, until a police dog named Gloria accompanies him when he gives his safety speeches. Students can give their own "safety speeches" and create "safety tips" to use not only in the classroom but school-wide.

Responsibility by Elain P. Goley (Rourke Enterprises, 1989). Using pictures and a very simple text, this book teaches the trait of responsibility to young children.

The Tale of the Vanishing Rainbow by Siegfried P. Rupprecht (North-South Books, 1989). A delightful fable about two kingdoms: the land of the bears and the land of the wolves. The lessons students learn from the kingdom are profound, including trust, peacefulness, harmony and friendship. (All ages.)

What If Everybody Did That? by Ellen Javernick (Children's Press, 1990). A child drops a can out the car window, talks during story time, splashes at the pool, and transgresses many other rules. After each infraction, he is asked: "What if everybody did that?" It's an excellent source to begin a class discussion on the need for rules.

When I Was Little by Jamie Lee Curtis (Harper Collins, 1993). This is a delightful four-year-old's memoir of her new-found capabilities. The repetitive refrain, "When I was little I . . . but now I . . .," is wonderful to use with younger students as they refer to beginning portfolio collections and then see evidence of their learning when compared to later selections.

Why Mosquitoes Buzz in People's Ears: A West African Tale by Verna Aardema (Dial Books, 1975). (Primary)

Intermediate Level or Advanced Listeners:
A More Perfect Union by Betsy and Giulio Maestro (Lothrop, Lee & Shepard Books, 1987). In wonderful pictorial form, this book describes how the greatest rules of our country (The Constitution) were drafted and ratified.

If I Were In Charge of the World by Judith Viorst (Macmillan 1981). Many teachers consider this compilation of poems written by a much-loved author to be a personal favorite. The forty-one poems reveal children's secret thoughts, worries and wishes, and are wonderful for discussions on rules.

Great Expectations by Charles Dickens (J.M. Dent, 1994). Here is the original story on the theme of "great expectations." Granted, the book is long and impossible to read aloud, but

> "Expect people to be better than they are; it helps them to become better. But don't be disappointed when they are not; it helps them to keep trying."
>
> —Merry Browne

there are many abridged editions now available as well as a newer movie version worth seeing (a few minutes on the concept of "great expectations" might be a perfect way to initiate the monthly theme.)

On My Honor by Marion Bauer (Clarion Books, 1986). This book contains a gripping tale of a child faced with accepting responsibility for his friend's death. (Advanced)

Nothing But the Truth by Avi (Orchard Books, 1991). This documentary novel won a well-deserved Newbery Honor medal. The story deals with a ninth grader who is suspended for not singing "The Star-Spangled Banner" during homeroom, an event which became a national news story. Avi's book is cleverly crafted and written entirely in memo, letter and script. It allows the reader to hear both sides of the story, since it is written from the point of view of both the teacher and student. The book allows for excellent discussions about topics such as the fairness of the main character's suspension and when rules are appropriate.

The Giver by Lois Lowry (Houghton Mifflin, 1993). Given his lifetime assignment at the Ceremony of Twelve, young Jonas becomes the receiver of memories shared by only one other individual in his community. In the process, he discovers the terrible truth about the society in which he lives. This Newbery Award-winning book is a gem! It is thought-provoking and can be used with an endless number of themes, including rules, memories, uniqueness and individuality.

The Book of Virtues, edited by William J. Bennett (Simon & Schuster, 1993). This book is an anthology of wonderful stories rich in moral literacy. The chapter on "Responsibility" is strongly recommended as a source of inspiring stories instructing children in the value of this critical Character Builder. This is a resource that should be on every teacher's shelf. (All)

The Summer of the Swans by Betsy Byars (Viking, 1970). A young girl must deal with the responsibility of caring for her disabled sibling. (Advanced)

Puppets

Please refer to pages 17–21, "How to Use Character Builder Puppets," for ways to use the puppet images.

Paper Bag Puppet

Duplicate the puppet head onto colored construction paper or cardstock-weight paper, cut out the shape and glue it to the front flap of a lunch-size paper bag. Features can be added to the face or body using items such as colored paper scraps, noodles, egg carton pieces, pipe cleaners, wall paper samples, yarn, bric-a-brac, and fabric.

ABLE RP1

SPARKY

SPARKY RP2

STINGER RP3

SUNSHINE RP5

SPINNER RP7

Permission to reprint for classroom use.
Character Builders, Jalmar Press
© 2000 by Michele Borba

RP9

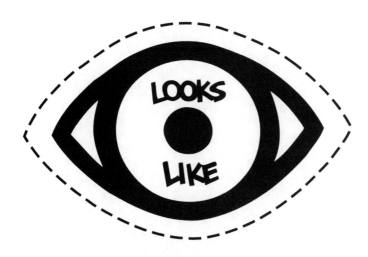

LOOKS LIKE

SOUNDS LIKE

RP9a

Worksheets, Activities, and Posters

ACCOUNTABILITY · DEPENDABLE · TRUSTWORTHY

Success
Through
Acting
Responsibly

I'M RELIABLE

I'M COMMITTED

I'M TRUSTWORTHY

I'M ANSWERABLE

I'M ACCOUNTABLE

RESPONSIBILITY

Doing what is right;
being accountable to yourself and others.

· COMMITTED · ANSWERABLE · ACCOUNTABILITY · DEPENDABLE · TRUSTWORTHY

RT1a **Responsibility Monthly Theme Poster**

Success
Through
Acting
Responsibly

RT1b

CARING

RESPONSIBILITY

CHARACTER BUILDER NOTEBOOK

RESPECT

COOPERATION & CITIZENSHIP

PROPERTY OF

_____

YEAR _____

RT1c

Permission to reprint for classroom use.
Character Builders, Jalmar Press
© 2000 by Michele Borba

Responsibility: response + ability

**Being answerable and dependable to others.
Doing what is right.**

   ## Looks Like

Sounds Like

HOW AM I RESPONSIBLE FOR WHAT HAPPENED?

WHAT COULD I DO NEXT TIME TO BE MORE RESPONSIBLE?

RT1d

Name _____ **Date** _____

Today's Topic: _____

_____

What I Think:

_____

_____

_____

_____

How I Feel:

RT1f

SOUNDS LIKE

Permission to reprint for classroom use.
Character Builders, Jalmar Press
© 2000 by Michele Borba

FEELS LIKE

RT1h

STARTERS AND STOPPERS

Character Builder: Responsibility:
"Success through acting responsibly."

**RESPONSIBLITY: Being answerable and accountable to
yourself and others. Doing what is right.**

RESPONSIBILITY PICTURES

RT2b

STOP IRRESPONSIBILITY PICTURES

RT2d

Name _____

Date _____

A Month of Responsibility

1. Number the days for this month.   2. Use these ideas as a guide for your daily journal writing.

MONDAY	TUESDAY	WEDNESDAY	THURSDAY	FRIDAY
What is one way you could be a more responsible student?	Look up the definition of responsible and write it down in your notebook.	Make a list of people you think are responsible.	Write a poem about why responsibility is important.	What are three ways you can show your teacher you are responsible?
Observe the characters on a half-hour TV show. Who was responsible? Who was irresponsible?	Learn to take three deep breaths and count to ten as a way to calm down. Practice at least 10 times.	List five ways you can show greater responsiblity for the environment.	Describe how to answer the phone in a responsible way.	What did the Framers of the Constitution do to take responsibility for the formation of our country?
List at least five synonyms for the word responsibility.	Cut out a newspaper or magazine article about a person who showed responsibility.	Write a word for each letter in the word responsibility that means almost the same thing.	List five antonyms for the word responsibility.	Find and/or draw 10 pictures of people acting responsibly. Paste them on paper to make a collage.
Write a paragraph describing how the world would be different if people showed responsibility.	Create a recipe for responsibility. What ingredients do you need?	Design a campaign button for responsibility.	Make a list of five ways you can be more responsible at home and five ways you can be more responsible at school.	Interview at least two adults to ask them to tell you five ways they show they are responsible at work.

RT3

Name _____ **Date** _____

A THOUGHT FOR THE DAY

Today's Date _____ **Today's Thought** _____

_____

My thoughts and ideas _____

_____

_____

Today's Date _____ **Today's Thought** _____

_____

My thoughts and ideas _____

_____

_____

Today's Date _____ **Today's Thought** _____

_____

My thoughts and ideas _____

_____

_____

RT5a

Name _____

Date _____

Responsibility Thoughts

1. Number the days for this month.   2. Use these ideas as a guide for your daily journal writing.

MONDAY	TUESDAY	WEDNESDAY	THURSDAY	FRIDAY
"Duty is the sublimest word in the language; you can never do more than your duty; you should never wish to do less." —Robert E. Lee	"You can't escape the responsibility of tomorrow by evading it today." —Abraham Lincoln	"A new position of responsibility will usually show a man to be a far stronger creature than supposed." —William James	"Responsibility for learning belongs to the student, regardless of age." —Robert Martin	"Few things help an individual more than to place responsibility upon him, and to let him know that you trust him." —Booker T. Washington
"We need to restore the full meaning of that old word, duty. it is the other side of rights." —Pearl Buck	"Make it a point to do something every day that you don't want to do. This is the golden rule for acquiring the habit of doing your duty without pain." —Mark Twain	"I leave this rule for others when I'm dead: Be always sure you're right—then go ahead." —Davy Crockett	"If we are ever in doubt about what to do, it is a good rule to ask ourselves what we shall wish on the morrow that we had done." —John Lubbock	"I believe that every right implies a responsibility; every opportunity, an obligation; every possession, a duty." —John D. Rockefeller, Jr.
"No snowflake in an avalanche ever feels responsible." —Stanislaw Jerzy Lee	"And so, my fellow Americans, ask not what your country can do for you: Ask what you can do for your country." —John F. Kennedy	"It is not fair to ask of others what you are not willing to do yourself." —Eleanor Roosevelt	"Taking responsibility means being aware of the multitude of choices you have in any given situation." —Susan Jeffers	"Responsibility: A detachable burden easily shifted to the shoulders of God, Fate, Fortune, Luck, or one's neighbors." —Ambrose Bierce
"In times like the present, men should utter nothing for which they would not willingly be responsible through time and in eternity." —Abraham Lincoln	"The responsibility of the great states is to serve and not to dominate the world." —Harry S. Truman	"Life has no meaning except in terms of responsibility." —Reinhold Niebuhr	"Liberty means responsibility. That is why most men dread it." —Maxims for Revolutionists	"Taking responsibility means never blaming anyone else for anything you are being, doing, having or feeling." —Susan Jeffers

RT 5b

Covenant

Name: _____
Date: _____

Responsibility Covenant

pledge
pact
oath
agreement
bond
contract
deal
promise
warranty
treaty
understanding
guarantee

Rules

Name: _____
Date: _____

OUR RULES ARE...WE USE CALM, 12" VOICES, WE LISTEN TO EACH OTHER

ordinance
law
decree
edict
statute
standards
doctrine
regulation
criterion
govern

arbitration
negotiation
resolution
principle
guideline
directive
policy
benchmark
gauge

Trustworthy

Name: _____
Date: _____

HOME WORK

believable
reliable
honorable
loyal
faithful
assurance
forthright
accountable
credible
dependable

Responsible

Name: _____
Date: _____

MAY I BORROW YOUR CRAYONS?

CRAYONS

obligation
promise
duty
commitment
guarantee
blamable
chargeable
accountable
liable
answerable

Name _____ Date _____

Responsibility Contract

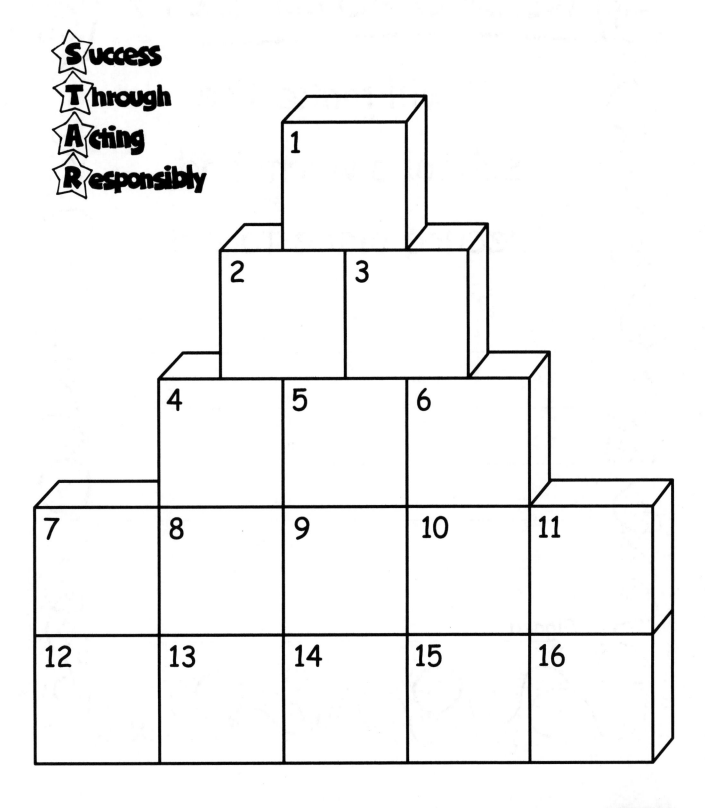

Success
Through
Acting
Responsibly

1

2   3

4   5   6

7   8   9   10   11

12   13   14   15   16

RT7

Vote for . . . RESPONSIBILITY

It will make the school a warm and secure place to be!

_____

_____

_____

_____

Signed _____

MEETING RULES

Raised hand = quiet.

Use a calm, 12" voice.

Listen attentively.

Extinguish putdowns.

Speak in turn.

RT8

Name _____ **Date** _____

MEETING NOTES

Topic: _____

Date: _____

_____

_____

_____

_____

_____

_____

_____

Topic: _____

Date: _____

_____

_____

_____

_____

_____

_____

_____

_____

_____

RT9

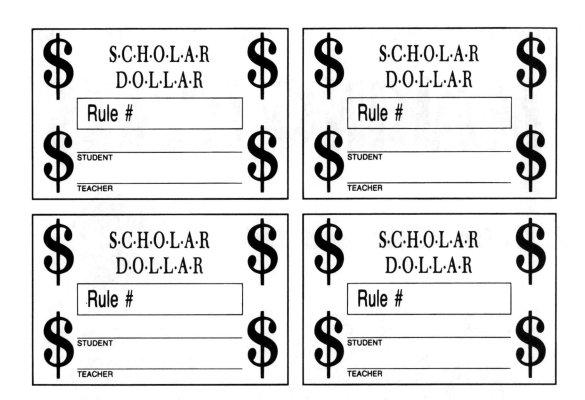

SCHOLAR DOLLAR WALLET

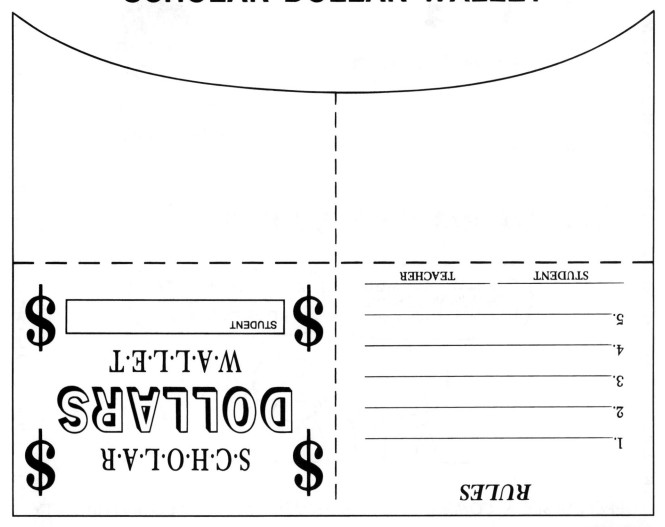

MAKING RULES

1. Calm down and think.

Take a slow, deep breath, stop

and then think!

2. Meet and make your rules.

RT12

BRAINSTORMING RULES

ALL IDEAS COUNT

NO PUT DOWNS

PIGGY BACK EVERYONE'S IDEAS

SET A TIME LIMIT

CHOOSE A RECORDER

RT13a

Responsibility Covenant

Covenant: an agreement, contract, promise or pact.

Responsibility: doing what is right; acting dependably.

1. _____
   _____
2. _____
   _____
3. _____
   _____
4. _____
   _____
5. _____
   _____
6. _____
   _____
7. _____
   _____
8. _____
   _____

Student _____

Teacher _____   Parent _____

PLEDGE SHAKE

1. Say the pledge.

2. Affirm your pledge and shake!

RT14

Responsibility Ticket

Awarded to _____

For _____

_____

_____

By _____

Date _____

⭐ **S**uccess
⭐ **T**hrough
⭐ **A**cting
⭐ **R**esponsibly

- -

Responsibility Ticket

I saw (name) _____ **in** _____ **(room no.)** acting responsibly today.

The responsible behavior was _____

_____

This was responsible behavior because _____

_____

Signed (name) _____ **your room no.** _____

Date _____

RT19

Permission to reprint for classroom use.
Character Builders, Jalmar Press
© 2000 by Michele Borba

Responsibility Award

This certificate is proudly awarded to

_____

in recognition of outstanding
effort in demonstrating

Responsible Behavior toward yourself and others.

Awarded this month of _____ 19____.

Authorized Signature _____

Congratulations!

Success
Through
Acting
Responsibly

Responsibility: Doing what is right;
being answerable and accountable for
your actions toward yourself and others.

The Responsibility of Self-Control

List ways you can be responsible for the emotional and physical safety
of others.

1. _____

2. _____

3. _____

4. _____

5. _____

6. _____

7. _____

8. _____

9. _____

10. _____

RT22a

STAYING CALM

1 + 3 + 10 = Calm

1 **Tell yourself: "Be calm!"**

+

3 **Slowly take 3 deep breaths.**

+

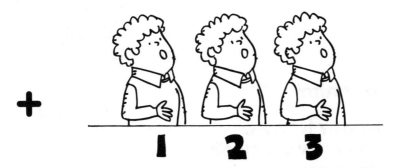

10 **Count slowly to 10.**

**I can act responsibly
by staying calm.**

RT27

CALMING DOWN

C   <u>C</u>ount to 10. Say: "Be calm."

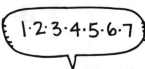

A   <u>A</u>sk: "What am I feeling?"

L   <u>L</u>ist ways to control self

- Walk away for now.
- Write or draw your feelings.
- Talk to someone.
- Count to 10.
- Take slow, deep breaths.

M   <u>M</u>ake a plan to stay in control. Do it!

RT28a

Permission to reprint for classroom use.
Character Builders, Jalmar Press
© 2000 by Michele Borba

SELF-CONTROL PLAN

C   Count to 10. Say: "Be calm."

A   Ask: "What am I feeling?"

L   List ways to control yourself.

M   Make a plan to stay in control. Do it!

C **To stay calm I will** _____

_____

_____

A **Ask: "What am I feeling?"** _____

_____

_____

L **List ways to control myself. What can I do?**

List To make it better I could:	*Consequences* If I did it, this might happen:
_____	_____
_____	_____
_____	_____

M **Make a plan to stay in control. Do it!**

_____

_____

_____

_____

_____

_____

RT28b

SELF-CONTROL PLEDGE

The next time I get angry and want to

_____

_____

_____

(the behavior I usually do that could get me in trouble)

and my body sends me these warning signals

_____

_____

_____

_____

(the warning signals my body sends me)

SWEATING
FLUSHED CHEEKS
CLENCHED HANDS
GRINDING TEETH
HEART POUNDING
???

I will

_____

_____

_____

(what I will do to stay calm)

NEXT TIME I START
TO GET OUT OF
CONTROL I WILL...

Signed _____

Date _____

Witness _____

Permission to reprint for classroom use.
Character Builders, Jalmar Press
© 2000 by Michele Borba

COOL AND CALM AWARD

Instructions:
Run off award on
construction paper,
punch a hole at top
and string yarn
through the hole.
The student "wears"
the award around
his or her neck.

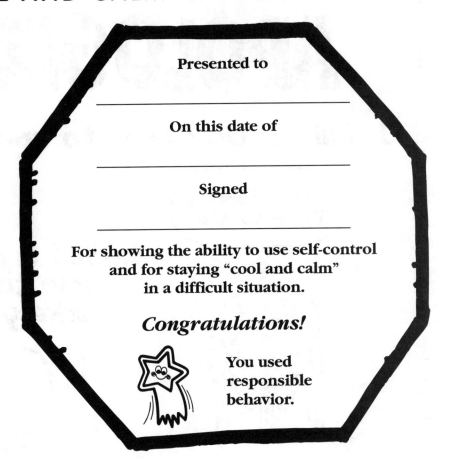

Presented to

_____

On this date of

_____

Signed

_____

**For showing the ability to use self-control
and for staying "cool and calm"
in a difficult situation.**

Congratulations!

You used
responsible
behavior.

Memo

Cool and Calm Award

Presented to

_____

On this date of

_____

Signed

_____

**For showing the ability to use self-control
and for staying "cool and calm"
in a difficult situation.**

Congratulations!

You used
responsible behavior.

RT30

APOLOGIZING

1. Think: "Do I need to apologize?"

2. Find a private time to sincerely make your apology.

3. Let the person know you are sorry.

RT31

Responsibility Phone Call Script

Please allow _____ to use the telephone to call his or her parents. Thank you!

Teacher's Signature _____ Date _____

Student's Phone Number _____

Date of Incident _____

Student Script to Parent

Hello, this is *(say your name)*. My teacher asked me to call you because today I did not act responsibly.

What I did was _____

_____

_____

This is against the school/class rules and my teacher asked me to talk with you about this.

Now talk with your parent about the problem.

I learned _____

_____

Next time I will _____

_____

to be more responsible. I will talk more about this at home with you later. I know I am responsible for my behavior. I will try to make a better effort to act responsibly.

Good-bye!

STUDY BUDDIES

> Rules for Study Buddies are use a calm, respectful, 12" voice, and no put downs.

> No interrupting. Look at the listener, eye-to-eye and listen to his message.

Ways to be a responsible study buddy partner:

Absences: Collect your buddy's assignments to catch him up.

Assignment check: Confirm assignments and due dates.

Study Partner: Review facts before a test.

Information: Clarify what the teacher said to your buddy.

Problem solving: Help your partner solve a problem.

Reading Partner: Read out loud to one another or help learn new words.

Proofreader: Check your partner's work for errors.

Support: Help your buddy have a successful day!

RT34a

Name _____ Date _____

Study Buddy Facts

Interview your Study Buddy. Write down your findings.

 Study Buddy's full name: _____

 Phone number: _____

 Address: _____

 Number of brothers and sisters: _____

 Pets: _____

 Birthdate: _____ Place of birth: _____

 Favorite TV show: _____

 Favorite book: _____

 Favorite movie: _____

 Favorite sport: _____

 Favorite color: _____

1, 2, 3 3 words that are usually used to describe you: _____

_____

 Hobbies and interests: _____

Name _____ **Date** _____

My Study Buddy

All about my Study Buddy:

Name: _____

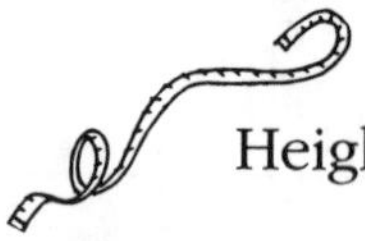

Height: _____

Hair: _____

Eyes: _____

Phone: _____

Likes to: _____

_____

Special talents: _____

_____

My Study Buddy fingerprints:

STAMP PAD

Right Thumb	Right Index	Right Middle	Right Ring	Right Little
Left Thumb	Left Index	Left Middle	Left Ring	Left Little

• TRUSTWORTHY • RELIABLE • COMMITTED • ACCOUNTABILITY •

DEPENDABLE • RELIABLE • ACCOUNTABILITY • ANSWERABLE • TRUSTWORTHY • COMMITTED

Name ______________________ **Date** ______________

1 : 3 : 1 Repair Sheet

The rule I broke is: ______________________

____

____

____

____

Things I could do to "fix it" so it won't happen again are: ______________

____

____

____

____

The one thing I will do to take the responsibility to "repair" the problem is:

____

____

____

____

Signed: ______________________

Repair Date: ______________________

Witness: ______________________

TRUSTWORTHY • RELIABLE • DEPENDABLE • COMMITTED • ANSWERABLE • ACCOUNTABILITY

• DEPENDABLE • COMMITTED • ANSWERABLE • ACCOUNTABILITY •

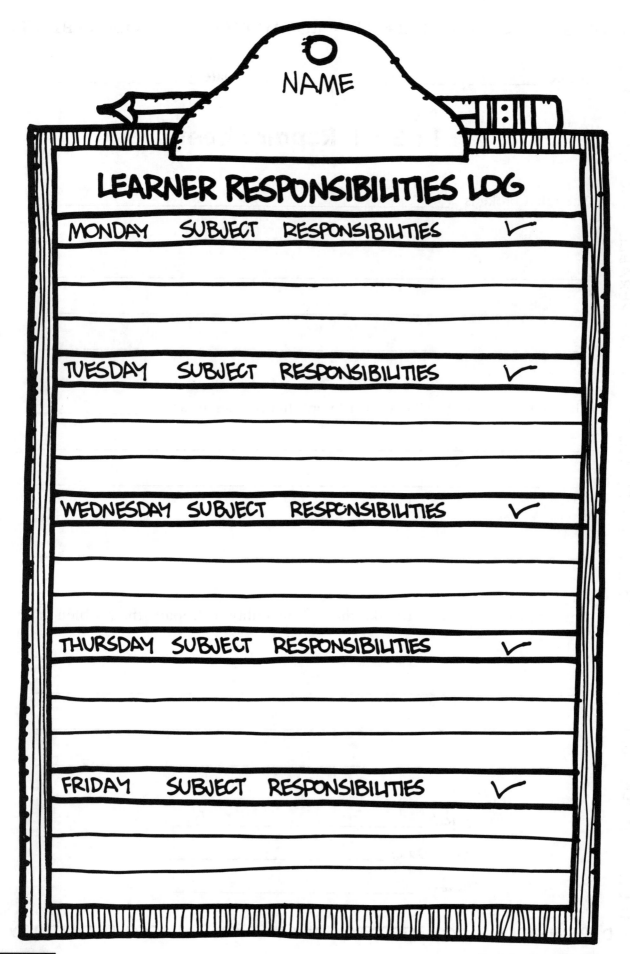

LEARNER RESPONSIBILITIES LOG

| MONDAY | SUBJECT | RESPONSIBILITIES | ✓ |

| TUESDAY | SUBJECT | RESPONSIBILITIES | ✓ |

| WEDNESDAY | SUBJECT | RESPONSIBILITIES | ✓ |

| THURSDAY | SUBJECT | RESPONSIBILITIES | ✓ |

| FRIDAY | SUBJECT | RESPONSIBILITIES | ✓ |

Permission to reprint for classroom use.
Character Builders, Jalmar Press
© 2000 by Michele Borba

Name _____ **Date** _____

Study Buddy Portfolio Evaluation

Directions: Choose one page in your portfolio that you think is your "best work." Now share your work with your Study Buddy and complete this evaluation together.

Title of Work or Project: _____

Date Evaluated: _____

My Comments: _____   Study Buddy's Comments: _____

_____   _____

_____   _____

_____   _____

Selection Criteria (Why this project was chosen.)

Me _____   Study Buddy _____

_____   _____

_____   _____

_____   _____

Strengths (What we liked about it.)

Me _____   Study Buddy _____

_____   _____

_____   _____

_____   _____

Suggestions for Improving (How to make it even better!)

Me _____   Study Buddy _____

_____   _____

_____   _____

_____   _____

Teacher Comments: _____

_____

_____

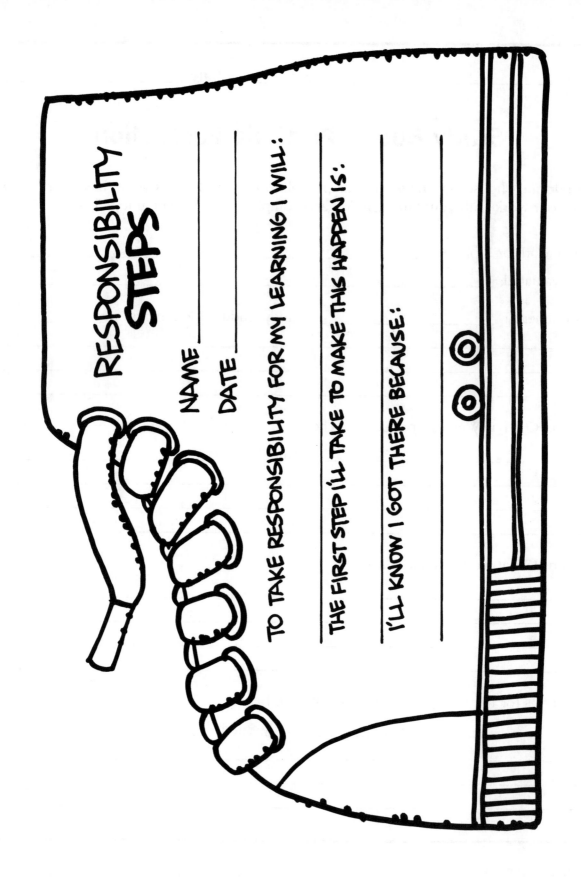

RESPONSIBILITY
STEPS

NAME _____

DATE _____

TO TAKE RESPONSIBILITY FOR MY LEARNING I WILL:
_____

THE FIRST STEP I'LL TAKE TO MAKE THIS HAPPEN IS:
_____

I'LL KNOW I GOT THERE BECAUSE:
_____

Name _____ Date _____

Responsibility Report

Responsibility: Being answerable and accountable.
Doing what is right.

A character you think acted responsibly: _____

Title: _____

Author: _____

Choose a way to show how the character was responsible:

Paint   *Draw*
Clay   *Cut and Paste*

Tell what the character did that was responsible: _____

_____

_____

_____

_____

_____

_____

Words to describe the responsible character:

_____ and _____

RT42a

Name _____   **Date** _____

Team Responsibility Report

Responsibility: Doing what is right; being answerable and accountable.

Team Members: _____   _____

_____   _____   _____

Responsible Character or Event: _____

_____

Resources	**Team Member**
_____	_____
_____	_____
_____	_____
_____	_____
_____	_____

Directions:

- Choose one character or event in history that your team thinks clearly demonstrates the trait of responsibility.

- Research your choice as a team. Each team member must read at least one resource about the character or event. You must use at least as many different resources as there are members in your team. All resources must be listed and then initialed by the primary team member who reads the source.

- Your team must then present to the class your conclusions about why you feel this character or event demonstrated responsibility. All team members must participate in the presentation.

- Presentation possibilities include:

A rap.	A play.	A skit.
A song.	A video.	A choral reading.
A poetry reading.	A puppet show.	Other? ASK!

Assigned team presentation date: _____

Permission to reprint for classroom use.
Character Builders, Jalmar Press
© 2000 by Michele Borba

Responsibility Projects

Directions: Choose any of the ideas below to create a project about responsibility. Show **WHAT** the trait means and **WHY** it is important to learn.

- mobile
- chart
- graph
- wind sock
- cube
- diorama
- movie
- puppet
- skit
- rap
- chant
- song
- rhyme
- cartoon
- poem
- play
- time line
- brochure
- news article
- want ad
- bumper sticker
- billboard
- headline
- relief map
- game
- backdrop
- transparency
- peek box
- banner
- newsletter
- photo album
- bulletin board
- interview

- tree map
- paper mache
- circle map
- spoke graph
- Venn diagram
- dance
- list
- charade
- calendar
- crossword puzzle
- letter
- advertisement
- display mural
- model
- debate
- painting
- pop-up book
- recipe
- riddle
- role play
- sculpture
- placemat
- motto
- survey
- media show
- maze
- mask
- hat
- paragraph
- scrapbook
- reader's theater
- pennant
- etching

- pamphlet
- constitution
- rubric
- stitchery
- ornament
- necklace
- oral report
- hanging
- commercial
- book jacket
- bookmark
- paper bag puppet
- jingle
- tongue twister
- tall tale
- myth or fairy tale
- menu
- campaign button
- telegram
- video
- mosaic
- book cube
- pantomime
- poster
- epitaph
- costume
- audio tape
- rebus
- journal
- announcement
- flag
- collage
- stamp

Name _____   Date _____

Responsibility Models

Directions: Choose any individual listed below or another person of your choice who you think is a model of responsibility. Be ready to tell the class WHAT the person did that demonstrated responsibility and HOW that action positively impacted others.

- Martin Luther King
- Mother Theresa
- Benjamin Franklin
- Scott O'Grady
- Jackie Joyner
- Wilma Rudolph
- Bonnie Blair
- Dan Jansen
- Allan Shepard
- Neil Armstrong
- Buzz Aldrin
- John Glenn
- Christa McAulfie
- Rosa Parks
- Anne Frank
- Abraham Lincoln
- Louisa May Alcott
- John Adams
- Michael Collins
- Susan B. Anthony
- Joan of Arc
- Ferdinand Magellan
- Mohandas Gandhi
- Isadora Duncan
- Lee Iacocca
- Colin Powell
- James Baldwin
- Shakespeare
- Oprah Winfrey
- Steven Speilberg
- Frank Lloyd Wright
- Maria Montessori

- Lewis and Clark
- Daniel Boone
- Louis Braille
- Andrew Carnegie
- Copernicus
- Marie Curie
- Vasco de Gama
- Charles Darwin
- John Kennedy
- George Washington
- Thomas Jefferson
- Charles Dickens
- Jimmy Carter
- Eleanor Roosevelt
- Cal Ripkin, Jr.
- Steve Fossett
- Monica Seles
- Michael Jordan
- Steve Young
- Harry Truman
- Charles Lindberg
- Anne Sullivan
- Wright Brothers
- Henry Ford
- Babe Ruth
- Nelson Mandela
- Ralph Emerson
- Ernest Rutherford
- Robert Frost
- David Livingston
- Thomas Beckett
- Alexander Graham

- Queen Elizabeth
- Albert Einstein
- Paul Revere
- Pocahontas
- Robert E. Lee
- Andrew Jackson
- Nat Turner
- Walt Whitman
- P.T. Barnum
- Jacqueline Onassis
- Helen Keller
- Gloria Steinem
- Ronald Reagan
- Theodore Roosevelt
- Jackie Robinson
- Frankline Roosevelt
- Jim Thorpe
- Sitting Bull
- Woodrow Wilson
- Jonas Salk
- Sally Ride
- Booker Washington
- Florence Nightingale
- Barbara Walters
- Amelia Earhart
- Dwight Eisenhower
- Walt Disney
- Thomas Edison
- Harriet B. Stowe
- George Lucas
- Charlie Chaplin
- Beethoven

RT42d

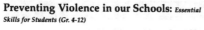